1 ²⁵

The Cabinet of
Curiosities

MUSEI
WORMIANI
HISTORIA

LUGD · BATAVORUM
EX OFFICINA ELSEVIRIANA
Acad Typog. 1655.

The Cabinet of Curiosities

Simon Welfare
and
John Fairley

St. Martin's Press
New York

Library of Congress Cataloging-in-Publication Data

Welfare, Simon.
    Cabinet of curiosities / Simon Welfare and John Fairley.
        p.   cm.
    ISBN 0-312-06919-7
    1. Curiosities and wonders.   I. Title.
    AG243.W443   1992
    031.02—dc20

                                                                                            91-36870
                                                                                            CIP

First published in Great Britain by George Weidenfeld & Nicolson Limited.

First U.S. Edition: February 1992
10 9 8 7 6 5 4 3 2 1

FRONTISPIECE
Danish physician Ole Worm's cluttered *Cabinet of Naturalia* in Copenhagen in 1655. Such
eccentric private collections of curiosities were the forerunners of modern museums.

Contents

Contents

Authors' Acknowledgements

Which section of the newspaper do you turn to first in the mornings? Sport? Business news? Foreign affairs? The important domestic issues of the day? We look at none of those. Instead, we eagerly scan the small paragraphs, usually tucked away at the bottom of the page, which report the latest weird and wonderful tales from a world that is always stranger than we can imagine. A few journalists specialize in collecting curiosities. Pre-eminent among them is Dermot Purgavie, whose 'America' column in the London *Daily Mail* we never miss.

The newspapers of the world contain something for our files almost every day. Our recent haul includes the theory, advanced by an American professor of psychology, that the themes of some of Mozart's greatest compositions were 'borrowed' from his pet starling. An account of the discovery of a barely decomposed human head in the belly of a tiger shark caught off Durban, South Africa, yielded this unforgettable quote from its captor: 'We found sections of human hair still stuck between the shark's teeth. It was sort of slobbery'. An enchanting photograph of two screaming babies in the arms of sumo wrestlers provided a new entry on our list of crazy contests: the infants were taking part in a 'how loud can you cry?' competition, held, according to the paper, 'throughout Japan to pray for babies' health'.

Among the friends who have monitored newspapers, magazines and scientific journals for us are John Lord in the USA, John and Lou Lidderdale in Canada, Adam Hart-Davis in the United Kingdom and Arthur C. Clarke in Sri Lanka. Sheila Fitzhugh and Sue Crofts and the Librarians of Aberdeen University and the London Library have located obscure publications. Others, including David and Marjorie Morgan, have lent us precious volumes from their collections. Philippa Braithwaite obtained supplies of rare publications from the United States. Expert advice was freely given by Paul Dunstan, Huon Mallalieu, Professor Stuart Piggott, Dr Keith Ross and Adam and Humphrey Welfare.

Wallace McRae of Forsyth, Montana, kindly gave us permission to reproduce his poem, 'Reincarnation'.

Once again, Melvin Harris has unstintingly allowed us to draw upon his vast knowledge of things mysterious and arcane.

We are grateful to them all.

Simon Welfare
John Fairley

The cabinet opens ...

One of the most ghoulish exhibits in any institution is a figure in the Royal Academy in London. It is the cast of the flayed body of a hanged man. With grim academic humour, he is known as 'Smugglerius' – because he was a smuggler.

The story is that he was one of two men who were hanged in London in 1775. The bodies were handed over for dissection to Dr William Hunter, the celebrated 'father' of modern surgery.

One criminal was duly cut up in front of the students. But when Dr Hunter came to the second man, he announced that the victim's muscular development was so remarkable that he did not wish to dissect him. So the corpse was carried to the Royal Academy Schools, where the sculptor Carlini had the body flayed and then placed in the attitude of the classical Roman statue of the Dying Gladiator. He then made a cast of his grisly artistic creation. Thus, the splendid muscles and bodily development which so fascinated Dr Hunter more than two centuries ago, survive to this day.

Fortunately for those with delicate stomachs, museums and galleries have changed greatly since Dr Hunter's time. Today, they are scientific and educational institutions devoted to the instruction and enlightenment of the public. In the eighteenth century and earlier, however, they existed simply as collections of curiosities: weird, wonderful, and sometimes grotesque objects amassed for their rarity value or oddity. In Germany they were known as *Wunderkammern*, in France as *cabinets des curieux*, in Britain as 'cabinets of curiosities'.

The often grisly collections of religious relics displayed in medieval churches were the forerunners of these bizarre hoards. England once boasted relics aplenty, as is shown by the list of trophies removed from churches and holy places between 1535 and 1540, during Henry VIII's campaign against the Roman Catholic Church. There were parts of bodies, such as 'Malchus' ear that Peter struck off,' and alleged souvenirs of the

'Smugglerius' from London's Royal Academy of Arts. The 'model' for this grisly showpiece was the flayed body of a hanged smuggler.

life of Jesus, including what was said to be a fragment of the manger at Bethlehem. The haul included 'St Peter's girdle', which had somehow found its way to Bath Abbey, while Bury St Edmunds yielded 'the coals that St Lawrence was toasted withal, the parings of St Edmund's nails, St Thomas of Canterbury's pen knife and his boots.'

Exhibits, almost as eccentric, covered virtually every square inch of the *Cabinet of Naturalia* established in Copenhagen in the seventeenth century by a Danish professor called Ole Worm. Here, as a famous drawing made in 1655 shows, natural curiosities such as a narwhal tusk, stuffed fish and birds, and exotic minerals, vied for the onlooker's attention with artefacts from far-off places. Worm's cabinet was typical of the age: a collection brought together by a person with an eye for the curious, with little attempt at scientific classification. A cabinet of curiosities was simply designed to excite wonder, to celebrate the marvellous strangeness of man and his world.

Sadly, the great cabinets were often dispersed on the death of their creators, but, in some cases, lists of their exhibits survive. Many were curious indeed. In Rome, for example, the *Wunderkammer* of a German scholar called Athanasius Kircher (1602–1680) contained 'monstrous eggs', 'a whole human body turned to stone', 'instruments used in ancient sacrifices,' 'a large collection of sea shells; among which, one called the Priest's Cap, is of such a venomous nature, that the least wound of it is mortal,' and examples of 'stones taken out of human bodies; particularly one weighing ten ounces, found in the bladder of *P. Leo Sanctius.*'

In London, in the seventeenth century, the 'Ark', a 'closet of rarities' formed by John Tradescant and his son, John the younger, contained 'flea chains of silver and gold with 300 links a piece and yet but an inch long,' 'two feathers of the Phoenix tayle,' 'Blood that rained in the Isle of Wight,' 'a bracelet made of thighes of Indian flyes,' – to name just a handful of the exotic exhibits. Don Saltero's coffee-house, one of the sights of the capital in the eighteenth century, boasted such doubtful oddities as a necklace formed from Job's tears and a straw hat said to have belonged to Pontius Pilate's wife's chambermaid's sister!

Some of the original cabinets eventually formed the nucleus of museum collections: the Tradescants', for example, was acquired by Elias Ashmole, who presented it to Oxford University in 1677. The Ashmolean Museum survives among the dreaming spires, and some of the Ark's prize exhibits can still be seen there in the Founder's Room.

At least one cabinet of curiosities has come down to us reasonably intact. Canon Bargrave's collection, in three small chests of drawers now kept in the library of Canterbury Cathedral, is packed with wonders. There are coins, an elaborately wrought false eye complete with 'optick nerve',

A true cabinet of curiosit[...]
made for Dr John Bargra[...]
in the 1660s (left), house[...]
the rarities he gathered [...]
his travels, including a
mummified finger from
France and a 'perfumed a[...]
stuffed' chameleon from
Africa.

North American Indian artefacts, a mummified finger and a 'perfumed and stuffed' chameleon. All were collected by Canon John Bargrave who travelled widely in the mid-seventeenth century, madly picking up curiosities on the way. For example, the mummified finger came from a crypt in Toulouse, France, which was full of preserved bodies. The visit was a memorable one: when the Canon playfully tweaked the dessicated hand of a soldier who had been stabbed to death, he noticed that 'the nerves and tendons were so strong that the hand returned with a lusty clap upon the wound.' The unfortunate chameleon was alive when Bargrave first acquired it in Algeria, but perished on the voyage home: a martyr to the Canon's eagerness to study its ability to change colour at the prod of a bodkin and to 'the lack of flies in the northern climes.' After more than three hundred years, its corpse, lovingly stuffed by the ship's surgeon, is a touching sight.

The strangeness of our planet has not diminished since the heyday of the cabinets, nor has the fascination of the curious. We like to think that this book is in the tradition of the enterprising Canon Bargrave and his fellow collectors. It is a celebration of the world's oddities, neither comprehensive nor analytical, but idiosyncratic and, above all, we hope, amusing.

Turn the page, and the doors of our cabinet of curiosities will open. Wonders await you.

1

Preposterous porkers

Pig-lovers pale at John Higgs's epitaph, inscribed on his tombstone in a Cheltenham cemetery:

> HERE LIES JOHN HIGGS
> A FAMOUS MAN FOR KILLING PIGS.
> FOR KILLING PIGS WAS HIS DELIGHT
> BOTH MORNING AFTERNOON AND NIGHT

Higgs obviously didn't realise what curious and clever creatures pigs are. In fact, talented pigs are a world-wide phenomenon. Recent reports tell of one, in Hot Springs, Arizona, USA, which learned to drive a Cadillac, and of some helpful hogs from Wales skilled in herding sheep. In Indianapolis, USA, a diminutive sow called Sadie, optimistically attired in a Hawaiian shirt, built up a reputation as a weather forecaster, while Cascade, Iowa, could boast of a 'stunt pig' named Lisa famed for her daring tricks. In Italy one happy hog named Fredo was thought capable of managing a fortune by his owner who left him a million, the Moscow State Circus regularly features hurdling pigs, while Durov's Corner, in the same city, likes to have a trained boar on its 'staff', and in Lüneburg, West Germany, one prescient porker managed to shoot the butcher who was about to turn him into bacon by tapping the trigger of his would-be executioner's gun with a well-aimed trotter. And if no one has yet persuaded a pig to fly, a Frenchman, the Abbé de Baigne, made several sing. In about 1475, the Abbé entertained King Louis XI of France with a 'consort of swine voices'. He built an 'organ' consisting of eight wooden boxes bolted together. Each contained a piglet. When he touched the keys, a spike would pop out and jab the 'singers', whose orchestrated squeals –

each pig had been chosen to 'sing' a different note – delighted king and courtiers. The Abbé was one of the first to realise how preposterous pigs can be ...

Luise – swine superstar

Luise, a 290-lb sow from Hildesheim, Germany, is known throughout the Federal Republic as *'das Media Hog'*. When not sniffing out drugs and explosives for the local police, Luise makes television appearances and sits for fashionable painters. In 1987 she became a film star, demonstrating her skills as a detective in *Blutrausch (Blood Frenzy)*. Said police trainer Werner Franke, the 'minder' of the 'sleuth on hoofs', 'My Luise has become almost immortal.'

Learned pigs

The 'Wonderful Pig', immortalised by the artist Thomas Rowlandson, was the sensation of London in 1785. He astonished the crowds who came to see him by apparently being able to read, solve mathematical problems, and spell out words. When the 'Amazing Learned Pig' died in 1788 and his master had departed to 'a madhouse' in Edinburgh, other 'sapient pigs' were ready to follow in his hoof-steps. One could apparently grunt in French, pronouncing, ' "*oui, oui*" with an uncommon fine accent.' Another, called Toby, is even said to have written his autobiography. His publicity material announced that 'THIS MOST EXTRAORDINARY CREA-TURE Will Spell and Read, Cast Accounts, PLAY AT CARDS; Tell any Person what o'Clock it is to a Minute BY THEIR OWN WATCH, ALSO TELL THE AGE OF ANY ONE IN COMPANY, And what is more Astonishing he will Discover a Person's Thoughts.'

Saved by a sow

In November 1984, the story of the brave Priscilla hit the American headlines. *USA Today* reported from Houston, Texas:

Priscilla, a pet pig who saved a child from drowning, will receive the American Humane Association's prestigious Stillman Award for

he 'stunt pig' performs
f her party pieces. 'She's
y unusual pig,' says
r Don Coohey, who
rds her with chocolate
'I've sent 100,000 to
ket over the last couple of
s, and she's the only one
s ever done stunts.'

super-sensitive snout has
ght fame to this German
, Luise, and many a drugs
on to justice.

heroism on Friday. The 7-month-old pig lives here with house painter Victoria Herberta, who taught Priscilla to swim last summer. On July 29 the pig was paddling around in a lake north-east of Houston when an 11-year-old retarded boy fell into the water. The child screamed, Priscilla swam toward him, the boy grabbed the pig's collar and she pulled him to shore. The child was coughing and the pig was squealing when human help arrived, but both were fine.

Pampered pets

Contrary to popular legend, pigs are clean and have made perfect pets. In the spring of 1987, three-month-old Truffles, owned by American-born country singer Cindy Jackson, took regular trots through London. 'There's nothing strange about walking a pig,' Cindy told a newspaperman. 'Truffles is just like a puppy dog really.'

A few years earlier, in northern Scotland, a much larger sow, called Twiggy, was given the freedom of the Stone family's beautiful eighteenth-century house near Tain, Ross and Cromarty. Among her many talents was a gift for mimicry: Twiggy quickly learned to imitate the family's dog and terrified the postman by barking. Coincidentally, another Stone family, from Santa Rosa, California, adopted a pig as a pet. Neal Stone found their Miss Piggy on a hunting trip, and within weeks she had made herself at home, watching television and crashing out on young Tony Stone's bedroom floor.

In North Carolina in 1986, neurosurgeon Ray Sattler and his wife Debbie gave a coming-out party for their debutante porker Norma Jean (named after Marilyn Monroe) and decked her in a pink tutu and diamanté earrings for the occasion. Don and Nola Schley of Elk Mound, Wisconsin, found that the idea that pigs are dirty creatures was, well, hogwash. They managed to housetrain Spot, their 485-pound brown-and-white 'baby', in just three days. 'He did have one "accident" indoors after being potty trained,' said Don. 'But I paraded him past the barbecue grill and showed him what a pork chop looks like – and he's been good ever since.'

Pig people

Many cases of 'wolf children' have been reported over the centuries, but the 'pig girl' described by a traveller named Wilhelm Horn in 1831 was a real rarity:

> [She was] a girl of twenty-two years of age, and by no means ugly, who had been brought up in a hog-sty among the hogs, and who had sat there for many years with her legs crossed. One of her legs was quite crooked, she grunted like a hog, and her gestures were brutishly unseemly in a human dress.

Even stranger were the 'pig-faced ladies' who were rumoured to have existed in Dublin and London at the beginning of the nineteenth century. Their grotesque features were gleefully portrayed in broadsheets and were the subject of much discussion amongst the curious. The most famous, indeed possibly the only authentic example of this curious breed, was Tannakin Skinker who was born two centuries earlier, in 1618, in Wirkham, a town on the River Rhine. Tannakin apparently communicated by grunting, and, although her parents tried to find her a husband in the belief that marriage would transform her into an ordinary woman, she is said to have failed to find true love.

The heavyweight hogs

Dr Julian Wiseman in his *History of the British Pig* publishes two pictures of gigantic porkers. One weighed 1,344 pounds and came almost up to his owner's shoulder, the other, an extraordinary rotund creature, clocked up 802 pounds at the age of two-and-a-half. Another heavyweight hog, all 1,410 pounds of him, was portrayed in a charming naive painting by Thomas Peplow Wood offered for sale at Sotheby's salerooms in London in 1986. The hog, a Gloucester Old Spot, was nine feet eight inches long and four feet eight inches tall, and lived in a village called Little Haywood in Staffordshire. The champion, as you might expect, comes from America, where 'Big Bill' of Henderson County, Tennessee, weighed in at 2,552 pounds. Bill, whose belly was so large that it touched the ground, went to the great sty in the sky in 1933, but his owners had him stuffed and proudly put him on display.

Trackstars from Heinold Hog Market seem to enjoy hoofing it round their 85-ft racecourse. 'Pigs are natural jumpers,' says their trainer. 'Put a hurdle between them and food, and they learn fast how to clear it.'

Swinedom's swiftest

'Swinedom's Swiftest' is the proud billing given to Robinson's Racing Pigs, one of America's two professional pig racing teams. The troupes are a major attraction at county fairs, where they run round an oval track. The winner takes all: a biscuit.

Robinson's, who started at the Florida State Fair in 1985, are comparative newcomers to the sport: Heinold Hog Market of Kouts, Indiana, began sponsorship of its teams in the late 1970s. According to the trainers, the pigs quickly learn what to do: Roy Holding of Heinold took just four days to train his original team. He did it by racing his 'athletes' to a food pan '20 to 25 times, three times a day. After four days, the pigs had figured out the game, and I'd lost five pounds.'

Both teams travel in luxurious trailers, as pampered as racehorses, and love the cheers of the crowd, 'The more you cheer for them the more they ham it up,' said one trainer. Another important factor: females are apparently better racers than males.

The sport of sows is catching on: at the Montgomery County Fair in Maryland, the pink and portly porkers dash round a 150-foot oval circuit at speeds of up to 10 mph in the annual 'Dash for the Mash'. In 1987 the exclusive Royal International Horse Show introduced pig racing to Britain. An expert, consulted by animal lovers, was not alarmed. 'Pigs like running about,' he was quoted as saying. 'It's not cruel as long as they are young.' The crowds loved the races; the horses, who traditionally shy away at the smell of pig, were apparently not so sure. But the sport has caught on. At Hackney City Farm in London, saddleback pigs regularly compete over a 100-yard course.

High sty-le

Finally, the most remarkable pigsty ever – one that, despite a few Egyptian flourishes, looks just like a Greek temple. It stands at Fyling Hall, near Fylingthorpe, North Yorkshire, and was commissioned in 1891 by a country squire desperate to improve the appearance of his gardens. (He apparently thought that if the place looked neat and somewhat magnificent his estranged wife might return to him.) The pigs took a less romantic view. They refused to trot up the ramp to their upstairs quarters, and it is thought that none of them ever took up residence there.

So it was not surprising that, by the 1980s, the building's glory had departed: its wooden Ionic columns had been riven by the English weather and repairs were needed. There was a danger that before too long it might look, well, like a bit of a pigsty. But help was at hand in the shape of the British government. The Department of the Environment agreed to list the 'temple' as a building of 'special architectural or historical interest,' thus making it eligible for repair grants and ensuring the future of one of the oddest agricultural buildings ever conceived. And 1988 saw the beginning of that future: the local council gave planning permission for the sty to be refurbished. Now tourists can spend their holidays in the palatial accommodation which the nineteenth-century pigs were unwise enough to turn down.

2

Lost!

In April 1987 there were red faces at America's National Archives. They had lost Dr Henry Kissinger's underpants. In 1978 the former Secretary of State had presented the boxer shorts, suitably inscribed, because, he said, the archivists were so acquisitive that they were trying to strip him down to his boxer shorts. And now they were nowhere to be found. Kissinger's underpants had joined the list of curious – and sometimes important and valuable – objects that have been lost without trace.

Mallory and Irvine's camera

Somewhere in the ice near the summit of Mount Everest, the bodies of two British climbers, George Mallory and Andrew Irvine, are thought to lie. And with them, perhaps perfectly preserved thanks to the cold, their Kodak camera which may contain photographs to prove that the world's highest mountain was conquered twenty-nine years before Hillary and Tenzing reached its summit in 1953.

Mallory and Irvine were last seen at 12.50 pm on 9 June 1924, only 800 feet from the summit. Everything appeared to be going well, but then the clouds obscured the two climbers from the view of their comrades below. They were never seen again.

Could their camera have survived? It is certainly possible, but several expeditions have searched in vain for it – and the photograph that might rewrite mountaineering history.

The island that turned turtle

When two turtle experts tried to visit Maziwi Island off Tanzania in 1982, they found that it had completely disappeared. The island had been the main nesting place for the turtles of the East African coast, and the researchers could find no trace of it nor of the rare Oliver Ridley turtle which had not been known to nest anywhere else in East Africa. One theory advanced to explain the island's disappearance was that fishermen may have blown it up while digging up coral and that a monsoon may have washed the debris away. The local people were alarmed, for according to legend, if Maziwi Island were to disappear, the world would come to an end.

Frances Scott Key's house

Frances Scott Key was the person who, in 1814, wrote *The Star Spangled Banner,* and is naturally a revered figure in American history. So when, in 1947, a highway was to be routed right through the modest house in Washington D.C. where Key wrote the song, the US National Parks Department was ordered to move it. To ensure the building could eventually be reconstructed on another site every inch of it was meticulously drawn and every brick numbered.

While they waited to discover where to re-erect the house, the Parks Department decided to store the pieces, which were therefore crated up and stored in a safe place. So safe, it turned out, that no one can remember where it is! Like the building itself, the plans and records have done a disappearing act, and all officials know is that the Key house is under a bridge somewhere. But which bridge and where? They are still looking.

The Irish Crown Jewels

The Dublin police have been searching for the Irish Crown Jewels since 6 July 1907 – the day they were found to be missing from the safe in the Bedford Tower of Dublin Castle where they were usually kept. Although, in fact, the missing gems were not Crown Jewels but the regalia of the Order of St Patrick, King Edward VII had planned to wear them during a visit to the city which had been due to start a few days after the robbery was discovered.

No trace of the Irish Crown Jewels – a diamond star, a collar studded with gems and adorned with roses and harps, and a diamond badge – has ever been found. From time to time since 1907 the hunt for the fabulous insignia – now certainly worth millions – has been revived, but the latest, in 1983, after a tip-off that they were hidden somewhere in the Dublin Mountains, came to nothing like all the others.

The bones of Peking Man

The finding of the fossilised remains of Peking Man in excavations near the Chinese capital in the 1920s and 30s was hailed as a breakthrough in the quest to understand how modern man may have evolved, for *homo erectus Pekinensis* lived some 800,000 years ago. Archaeologists had collected the remains of about forty Peking people when excavations stopped at the onset of the Second World War. During the Japanese invasion of China, the precious fossils were crated up and put on a train, but they did not reach safety. The train was searched by the invaders and the bones were never seen again. All that remains are some casts of the fossils, the excavation drawings – and a single authentic tooth which one of the archaeologists had kept for himself, and strung on his watch chain.

Dante's ashes

In the Spring of 1987 worried officials of the National Library in Florence mounted a search for two sealed envelopes said to contain some of the ashes of Italy's greatest poet, Dante Alighieri (1265–1321), author of the *Divine Comedy*.

Dante was always thought to have been buried in Ravenna where he settled in about 1318 after being exiled from Florence, but some of his ashes were apparently acquired by a certain Atto Vannucci, one of the poet's devoted followers. Vannucci gave them to Enrico Pazzi, the sculptor of Dante's monument in the church of Sante Croce in Florence, and he presented them, in the two envelopes, to the National Library at around the turn of the century. They were last seen in 1935.

Where had they got to and did they really contain Dante's ashes or merely chippings from Dante's sarcophagus as the director of the National

Library suggested during the 1987 search? Embarrassed officials were hunting high and low for the envelopes and the answer, when suddenly an urn containing Dante's ashes turned up in the senate building in Rome – which suggests that Dante, like Gaul, was divided into at least three parts. One in Rome, one in Ravenna, and one somewhere in Florence – but where?

Treasures

The lure of hidden treasure is a heady one, so to find a haul of gold or precious jewellery and then to lose it again is a bitter experience indeed. Here are some golden hauls which have disappeared in curious circumstances.

The **Hen and Chicks**, which probably dated from the fourth century, were a casualty of war. They were found with a hoard of Visigothic treasure in 1837 near a Romanian village by two quarrymen, and passed through many hands before ending up in a museum in Bucharest. In 1875, the treasure was stolen but later recovered by police. However, it then disappeared from Iasi, Moldavia, where it had been sent for safe keeping at the time of the Russian Revolution.

The **Dorak Treasure** is one of the greatest enigmas of modern archaeology. Its discovery, announced in 1959 in the *Illustrated London News*, caused excitement not simply because the hoard apparently came from ancient royal tombs unearthed near the village of Dorak in Turkey and contained rare figurines, ceremonial battle-axes, fine jewellery, swords, daggers, a magnificent gold cup, and a throne covered with a layer of gold and hieroglyphs, apparently a gift from an Egyptian king. What intrigued the archaeologists were the circumstances of the discovery. The story is controversial to this day.

The find was reported by James Mellaart, then Assistant Director of the British Institute of Archaeology in Ankara. He said that while travelling through Turkey in the summer of 1958 he met a pretty girl on a train. Even more striking than her looks was the gold bracelet she wore on her wrist. It looked very old.

The girl confirmed Mellaart's hunch. The bracelet was indeed ancient, part of a treasure trove. She had the rest at home. He was welcome to see it. So when they reached Izmir, Mellaart left the train and went to the

A GODDESS AND HER HANDMAIDENS—IN UNIQUE FIGURINES OF 4500 YEARS AGO.

   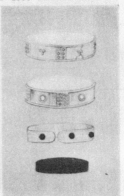

FIG. 2. THE TWO BRONZE FIGURINES PRIEST-ESSES OR WORSHIPPERS WEARING WHAT WAS PRESUMABLY THE NORMAL DRESS OF THE VORTAN RULING CLASS (6 INS. HIGH).

FIG. 3. BACK VIEW OF FIG. 2. THE FIGURES ARE OF BRONZE WITH SILVER GARMENTS; AND HAIR, ORNAMENTS AND DECORATION IN GOLD. TWO HAIRSTYLES ARE SHOWN.

FIG. 5. ONE OF THE ATTENDANTS ON THE GODDESS. THE BODY IS ENTIRELY MADE OF SILVER, THE HAIR AND ALL THE ORNAMENTS BEING GOLD.

FIG. 6. PERSONAL JEWELLERY FROM THE QUEEN'S TOMB: GOLD AND SILVER BRACE-LETS, WHOSE PATTERN MAY ALSO BE OBSERVED ON THE FIGURINES.

FIG. 7. THE GODDESS (RIGHT) IN ELECTRUM AND HER PRINCIPAL ATTENDANT IN SILVER, ALL THE ADDITIONAL ORNAMENTS BEING IN GOLD. THE GODDESS'S GOLD BELT AND PENDANTS ARE SOLDERED ON BUT THE "GRASS SKIRT" IS ENGRAVED. LIFE SIZE.

FIG. 8. THE BACK VIEW OF THE TWO FIGURINES SHOWN IN FIG. 7. THE SILVER FIGURE, WEARING A GOLD-EDGED SILVER APRON, HOLDS A CIRCLET, WITH SEVERAL BIRDS ON IT. PERHAPS A MUSICAL INSTRUMENT OF THE SISTRUM TYPE.

It is not absolutely certain that these five amazing figurines in electrum, silver and bronze were actually found in the two tombs; and Mr. Mellaart, while convinced of their genuineness, thinks that they may be a little later. All are about 6 ins. high, cast in a two-piece mould and are naturalistic though a little flat. All the articles of dress, hair, necklaces, bracelets and anklets were made in sheet gold or wire and were added by soldering or sweating-on, or, in some cases, loosely fixed. It is noteworthy that the objects of jewellery are exactly to be paralleled among the jewellery found with the queen in the double tomb; and Fig. 6 shows a group of bracelets from that tomb—two of them were found round the queen's arms—which exactly resemble the bracelets worn by the figurines. There seems little doubt that the electrum figure represents the goddess, the two silver figures her close attendants and the bronze figures her priestesses or worshippers. The silver figurine in Fig. 8 is especially interesting. It is suggested that the rod in the left hand was used to beat the bird-studded circlet in the right hand to produce a musical note. One of the bronze figures holds a similar circlet.

e sketches published by *The Illustrated London News* in 1959 are the only visual record of the mysterious k Treasure. Among the rare artefacts a British archaeologist claimed to have seen were these five zing figurines'.

girl's house where she showed him not only other artefacts but also photographs of the tombs, complete with skeletons, in which they had been found. As so often happens when mysteries are under investigation, there was no opportunity to take photographs: Mellaart's camera was broken. Instead, the archaeologist stayed on for three or four days, recording as much detail as possible in his notebooks.

Those sketches and Mellaart's testimony are virtually the only evidence that the Dorak treasure ever existed. All efforts to trace the girl later – she said her name was Anna Papastrati – came to nothing. Even the house which Mellaart claimed to have visited could not be identified with any certainty. The Dorak treasure seems to have disappeared as mysteriously and as suddenly as it came to light.

At least two other great treasures, now lost, are tantalisingly 'preserved' through drawings made at the time of their discovery.

The first is a magnificent Anglo-Saxon jewelled silver hanging bowl, found in the River Witham near Lincoln, and described by one expert as 'the most remarkable piece of pre-Conquest plate ever found in England'. During the nineteenth century the bowl was in the collection of a collector of antiquities named John Heywood Hawkins, but its whereabouts have been unknown since then. Indeed, modern experts only realised the Witham Bowl had ever existed when a drawing of it was found in a scrapbook in the library of the Society of Antiquaries of London.

The second is the Sark Hoard, discovered in the Channel Islands at the beginning of the eighteenth century. In this case, too, drawings of the treasure turned up in the Society of Antiquaries' library. These make it abundantly clear that the Sark Hoard was quite a find.

It had come to light when five islanders were digging a farm ditch. However, they were forced to surrender it to the authorities as the result of a court case in which one of the discoverers was found guilty of allowing his dog to run loose. For this, to modern eyes, minor offence, the Procurator imposed a painful fine: the Sark Hoard had to be handed over.

The hoard, possibly hidden in around 50 BC – the time of Caesar's conquest of Gaul – was of Thracian origin and would now be of immense value: it included a silver gilt mount decorated with fishes, thirteen round silver, or silver-gilt, discs embossed with animal designs, eighteen silver coins, and the iron-bound pot in which it had been hidden.

Nothing has been heard of the Sark Hoard since 1727, when it was in the possession of the Earl of Hertford, later 7th Duke of Somerset. So if you happen to have it in your attic or on your sideboard, there are plenty of people who would like to know ...

Cromwell's body

The fate of Oliver Cromwell's body proves that it does not pay to overthrow the King of England if you wish to be honoured after your death. Cromwell died on 3 September 1658, and the corpse of the man who had King Charles I executed suffered all kinds of indignities. It was secretly buried in London's Westminster Abbey, and a wooden effigy dressed in magnificent robes substituted for the lying-in-state and public funeral. Then it was exhumed in 1661 after the Restoration and the grisly remains displayed for a day on the gallows at Tyburn. What happened next is a mystery. The body was cut down at sunset and thrown into a pit which was somewhere near the site of the present-day Connaught Square. But was it Cromwell's, or had another corpse been substituted? Rumours were rife, and one legend has it that the real body was smuggled out of London and buried at Naseby. Leicestershire, scene of Cromwell's greatest victory.

And talking of Cromwell's mortal remains, we can't resist the opportunity to tell you about his head. The one certain fact about it is that it was severed from that peripatetic body and displayed on the southern gable of Westminster Hall for about twenty-five years before vanishing. From then on, still impaled on its iron spike, it pops up ghoulishly from time to time:

- in a private museum in London owned by a tycoon called Mr DuPuy.

- in the hands of a down-and-out actor called Samuel Russell who tried to sell it to Cromwell's old Cambridge college, Sidney Sussex, in 1775.

- on sale in Bond Street, London, in 1799.

- on exhibition at the Royal Archaeological Institute, London, in 1911.

- under examination by two scientists who pronounced it genuine after checking against portraits of Cromwell and establishing that its size matched that of his helmet.

- bequeathed in the will of its eventual owner, Canon Wilkinson, to Sidney Sussex College. In 1960 it was buried there in a secret grave so that it might, after its travels, rest in peace.

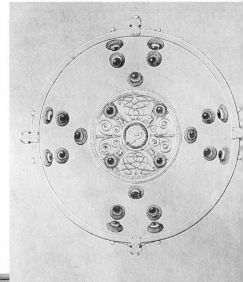

Two lost treasures: the Witham bowl (right), last seen in the collection of an antiquarian who died in 1877; and the Sark Hoard (below), described by archaeologists as 'one of the most exciting hoards of treasure found in British territory,' which disappeared in the eighteenth century.

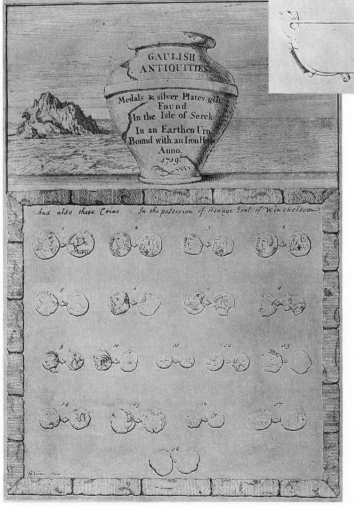

GAULISH ANTIQUITIES

Medals & silver Plates &c Found In the Isle of Serck In an Earthen Urn Bound with an Iron H Anno. 1719.

And also these Coins. In the possession of Henage Earl of Winchelsea

The missing manuscript

The legendary Lawrence of Arabia claimed that he lost his only copy of the first eight 'books' of *The Seven Pillars of Wisdom* in a railway refreshment room in Reading in December 1919.

So much legend surrounds Lawrence of Arabia, that it is now difficult to determine the exact truth, but the tale of the missing manuscript certainly adds a romantic footnote to one of the greatest swashbuckling stories of the twentieth century. And Lawrence's manuscript is by no means the only one to have gone missing before another copy could be made.

Thomas Carlyle unwisely lent the original of the first book of his *French Revolution* to John Stuart Mill. It had taken Carlyle five months to write, but he somehow managed to conceal his dismay when Mill confessed that the manuscript had been accidently destroyed by a servant. Always short of money, Carlyle reluctantly accepted the hundred pounds in compensation – and began all over again.

British writer Jilly Cooper put down the first draft of her novel *Riders* in a London store in 1971 – and that was the last she saw of it. 'I had been to a particularly boozy lunch in Selfridges,' she later wrote, 'and I left the whole of the first draft of my book *Riders* there. It was just about to be published and I didn't have a copy of a single word. Of course, it never turned up and I didn't get it together again until 1985 – fourteen years later.'

Better, perhaps, to lose your manuscript completely than to suffer the fate of the sole copy of Swedish business consultant Ulf af Trolle's learned work on his country's economy. Prudently, Mr Trolle arranged to have photocopied the 250 pages he had taken thirteen long years to write. But an assistant at the firm he went to confused a copier with a shredder. The result? 50,000 strips of paper and an aghast author, who, after the initial shock, stoically settled down to try to stick them all together.

Jean Mitry, who died in January 1988, was a distinguished French film critic, director and historian. Thanks to a simple name change, he succeeded in making people forget his real name which was Jean-René-Pierre Goetgheluck Le Rouge Tillard des Acres de Presfontaines, but no one ever forgot how he lost a crucial part of one of the greatest of all French films. Indeed, Gilbert Adair's obituary of Mitry in London's *Independent* began with the sorry tale:

> *La Nuit du Carrefour* (*A Night at the Crossroads*), made in 1931, adapted from a Simenon novel and featuring the director's brother Pierre as Inspector Maigret, is one of Jean Renoir's most enigmatic but beautiful

and dream-like films, fascinating for its innovatory use of natural sound and location shooting. Yet the mystery at the heart of the film, a mystery rendering its narrative so elliptical as to be almost incomprehensible – its essential *modernity*, in other words – derived less from the who-dunnit conventions of Simenon's plot or any conscious experimentation on Renoir's part than from the fact that two reels of the original, irreplaceable negatives, were unaccountably lost by the director's friend and collaborator Jean Mitry.

D.B. Cooper's haul

When they're not searching for Bigfoot, the elusive apeman said to inhabit America's Pacific Northwest, the people of the Cascade Mountains on the Washington-Oregon border join the seemingly never-ending quest for D. B. Cooper's haul.

The story began in Portland, Oregon, in November 1971, when a man who checked in as Dan Cooper took Northwest's flight 305 to Seattle, Washington. During the journey, Cooper handed a note to a stewardess. It said he had a bomb in his briefcase and that he would detonate it if his orders were not obeyed. When the plane reached Seattle, he called for $200,000 and four parachutes. These were put on board, the money in the bag weighing 21 pounds.

After all the passengers and some of the crew had been released, the plane flew on. It was night, and the outside temperature was well below zero. No one saw Cooper leave, but it is thought he jumped from the Boeing 727 over Ariel, Washington, taking the loot and two of the parachutes with him.

Nothing definite has been heard of D. B. since, although hundreds of people have 'confessed' to his crime. Almost a decade after Cooper's disappearance scraps of money were found twenty-five miles south of Ariel and authenticated as part of his booty. A parachute was also found in the area some years later. Yet no trace of the man himself has ever been found. Many believe he did not survive to enjoy any of his ill-gotten gains: he may have died as he hit the ground, or in the bitter cold of that November night. Whatever D. B. Cooper's fate, whoever he really was, his crime has become an American myth, and every year, around the anniversary of his death, in the Pacific Northwest the mountain people swap theories, scratch their heads in wonder, and remember him.

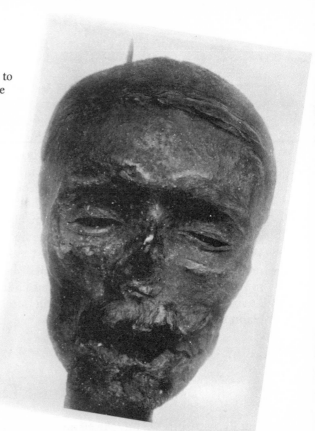

...er Cromwell's severed head which had to
...t more than 300 years for burial. Note
...remains of the famous wart over his right
...brow and the spike on which his head
...impaled outside Westminster
...in 1661.

...ow Winna Winfried (left) and Pierre
...oir (centre) in *La Nuit du Carrefour*.
...of the film makers lost two original
...s, but this seems only to have
...ed to the movie's charm.

The Frenchman who lost his bottle

Somewhere on an island off the shores of Western Australia a bottle lies buried, and with it one of the 'ifs' of history. It was apparently hidden by a Frenchman called Saint Allouarn who made a landfall on the continent in 1772, after his ship, the *Gros Ventre*, had drifted in fog during an expedition to the Antarctic. Captain Cook had discovered Australia two years earlier and had laid claim to what is now New South Wales in the south-east. The Frenchman, however, claimed Western Australia or, as he apparently put it in the message he left in the bottle, 'the land of Western New Holland in the name of the King, Louis XV'. But the French never pursued their claim and the British prevailed. Modern expeditions to Dirk Hartog Island, the place where Saint Allouarn buried the bottle, have so far failed to locate the missing parchment on which the territorial claim was written.

Where are you J. D. Starkey?

Finally, someone we have tried and frustratingly failed to locate: a traveller with a remarkable story to tell. In 1980 we were making the television series *Arthur C. Clarke's Mysterious World,* starring, you won't be surprised to hear, the world's foremost writer on science.

Our researchers turned up an extraordinary description in a magazine article of an encounter with a truly gigantic squid, estimated at more than 175 feet long, with tentacles 2 feet thick. The eyewitness, according to the article, was a certain J. D. Starkey. He had seen the monstrous creature from the deck of an Admiralty trawler off the Maldives by the light of a cluster of bulbs which he had lowered into the water. He wrote:

> As I gazed, a circle of green light glowed in my illumination. This green unwinking orb, I suddenly realized, was an eye. Gradually I realized I was gazing at almost point-blank range at a colossal squid – the body alone filled my view as far as my sight could penetrate. I am not squeamish, but that cold, malevolent, unblinking eye seemed to be looking directly at me. I don't think I've ever seen anything so coldly hypnotic and intelligent before or since.

When we made inquiries, no one seemed to know who Starkey was. Now it may seem immodest to say so, but few people escape the expert sleuthing of our researchers, yet J. D. Starkey eluded us. It rankles still. We would like to know more; to hear the description of this wondrous beast from Starkey's own lips – if he is still alive to tell the tale. The only thing that bothers us is that Starkey is the name of a famous seaman in English fiction, one of the comic characters in J. M. Barrie's *Peter Pan* . . .

3

Found!

This section should give hope to people hunting for the lost objects in the previous one, for all kinds of curious things thought to have disappeared for ever have turned up again. Sometimes they have been exactly where they should have been all the time. For example, in the early 1980s, Washington's Smithsonian Institution spent $5 million on cataloguing the 22 million items in its collection. No one was in the least surprised when the list revealed the whereabouts of some prize exhibits that had not been seen for ages – including President Eisenhower's pyjamas, a tomahawk once owned by Davy Crockett, a Civil War soldier's shoes (size 18) and some underwear once worn by an astronaut. These interesting pieces of Americana weren't really lost, of course, simply uncatalogued, but here are some 'lost' things which have turned up in the strangest circumstances.

The King, the cup and the collar studs

When the Rillaton Gold Cup, an important Bronze Age treasure found in Cornwall in 1837, was rediscovered in 1936 after disappearing for decades from public view, it was full of collar studs!

In 1982, a British archaeologist Professor Christopher Hawkes described the cup's strange odyssey from dig to dressing-table. Because it had been found on royal property, the cup was sent to King William IV, who was deemed to be the rightful owner. Later, in the 1850s, Prince Albert displayed it in his Family Museum at Osborne, Isle of Wight. By the reign of George V, however, it had disappeared from view. On the King's death in 1936, worried archaeologists and museum curators made discreet inquiries.

One of them showed Queen Mary an engraving of the cup. Yes, she thought she did remember it, and off she went to Windsor Castle where she was able to lay hands on the exquisite Bronze Age cup immediately. It was sitting on her late husband's dressing-table: he had always kept his collar studs in it. A word to the new King, Edward VIII, and the Rillaton treasure was deposited in the British Museum. The fate of the collar studs is unknown.

In the oddest places

The story of the Rillaton Gold Cup is a reminder that treasure can be found in the most unlikely places.

In the mid-1980s, the long-lost original of one of the cinema's greatest masterpieces, *La Passion de Jeanne D'Arc*, made by Carl Dreyer in 1928, turned up in the **cellar of a psychiatric hospital** near Oslo, Norway.

A farmer in Northumberland was intrigued when he found a strange little wooden figure of a woman in a **drawer** at his farm. It was shown to an expert who, puzzled, sent a photograph of it to a colleague in London. The expert knew exactly where it must have come from: the island of Fiji. He also knew it was rare – only five other examples were known. Of these, three were in New Zealand museums and a fourth was in Cambridge. The farmer's figure fetched £33,000 at auction in 1986.

The ashes of Dorothy Parker, who enlivened the New York literary scene in the 1920s with her wit and exquisite bitchiness, were discovered in a **filing cabinet** in 1987. They got there because, after Parker died twenty years earlier, no one could decide what to do with her ashes. So they were looked after by the writer Lillian Hellman, and, when she died, were passed on to her lawyer for safe keeping. The discovery reopened the controversy about where Miss Parker's last resting-place should be. Some of her fans asked for the ashes to be divided up into little parcels and given to them; an artist suggested painting the ashes into a portrait of Parker 'to use my talent to recognise and memorialise her for her talent'; there was even a suggestion that they should go on a nationwide 'farewell tour' in aid of charity! Eventually, however, it was decided that the ashes should be scattered in a memorial garden in Baltimore. Parker, who has always been identified with New York, would surely have had something to say about that.

A pair of hunting pistols, decorated with ivory and gold, made for the

A pair of pyjamas once owned by President Dwight D. Eisenhower is one of more than 22 million items Americana preserved at the Smithsonian Institution in Washington, DC.

The Rillaton Gold Cup. King George used to keep his collar studs in this exquisite example of Bronze Age craftsmanship.

Russian Empress, Catherine the Great (1729–1796), somehow got into the **New York Police Department's vault** in 1982. In fact, the last stage of its odyssey was known: the pistols, made by the imperial gunmaker Johan Adolph Grecke and valued at $200,000, had been seized during a drugs raid in the South Bronx some years earlier, and were only noticed when they were sent for destruction with a vast haul of illegal weapons amassed by the cops. But how they had got to the South Bronx was a mystery that baffled even the sleuths of the NYPD.

It's always wise to be wary of a **cardboard box**, for the grisliest things can be packed in them. Parts of the brain of scientist Albert Einstein, for example, were kept in glass jars in a box labelled 'Costa Cider' (see page 115). And in the 1980s, the death mask of Pancho Villa, the Mexican revolutionary assassinated in 1923, turned up in a similar box at a school in El Paso, Texas.

A court case was recently fought in New York over the ownership of $17,000 found hidden between sheets of lasagna in a **deep freeze** on Long Island in the United States. The cash was said to have been pilfered from a suitcase containing $5 million which was deposited in a Manhattan warehouse by a Hungarian doctor in the 1920s. But after the doctor's death no claimant could be found, and the fortune mouldered in the case for almost half a century. The court wrangle was between the warehouse owner and the police pension fund for the relatively small amount of cash that could be located (both in the lasagna and elsewhere) after the case's contents had been 'fingered' by two of the warehouse employees and an accomplice. They were found guilty of theft in a separate trial.

The manuscript of poet and playwright Dylan Thomas's masterpiece, *Under Milk Wood*, was found in a **London pub** by BBC radio producer Douglas Cleverdon after Thomas had mislaid it during a pub crawl. If an over-zealous cleaner had consigned the script to the dustbin or the fire, one of the greatest dramatic works ever created for radio would have been lost for ever.

In the early 1970s, an important and valuable section of a frieze dating from Classical times turned up in a niche in a **folly** at Fawley Court, near Henley-on-Thames. The marble sculpture, known as 'the fallen giant', was carved between 182 and 165 BC and formed part of the great altar at Pergamon, a city in Asia Minor. The rest finished up in East Berlin. Like so many of the treasures of the Classical world, the marble slab was originally acquired by an English nobleman, Thomas Howard, Earl of Arundel (1585–1646), while travelling in Italy.

Pots of money

Valuable Ming vases are always turning up in odd places. Vivian and Elizabeth Clement of Glasgow, Scotland, were visiting the city's renowned Burrell Collection of art when they noticed a vase just like the one that formed the base of a lamp they had at home. Vivian had inherited it from an uncle who had picked it up in a junk shop for £10 in 1945. The Clements took their vase to an expert who identified it as fourteenth-century Ming. It sold for £390,000.

In 1981 George Cottrell, a retired builder from Oxfordshire, got far less for his Ming vase – £16,000 – but then it wasn't in as good condition as the Clements' lamp. For George had found it in pieces in a yard on his land – its previous owner had obviously thrown it out as rubbish – and had painstakingly reassembled the pot like a jigsaw. Said an auction house expert, 'For an amateur, his restoration was an excellent job.' George, who attended the sale with his daughters and saw his jigsaw knocked down to an eastern buyer, was quite philosophical. 'We will be sorry to see the vase go,' he said, 'but you cannot have the pot and the money.'

Saleroom surprises

A rediscovered masterpiece always lends drama to the already theatrical atmosphere of an auction. Here's a pair that was apparently lost to art-lovers only to be triumphantly restored to public prominence in the saleroom.

In April 1986 six nineteenth-century paintings of pigs which had been bought in the 1930s for ten shillings fetched £44,800 at an Edinburgh auction. For years they had lain unloved in a garden shed in Dumfriesshire, Scotland. Not surprisingly, the owner was said to be 'in a state of shock' when she realised what valuable treasures had been knocking about in the shed along with the flower-pots and the garden tools. Two of the pictures, by the way, had an added curiosity value. They were painted by John Vine, who specialised in farm pictures. Vine was born with a handicap not likely to encourage anyone to become an artist: his arms were so deformed that he was exhibited as a fairground freak. Yet he worked out a way of holding a brush and is now a sought-after master of primitive painting.

A book called *The Gospels of Henry the Lion* had not been seen since the late 1930s when it surfaced in a London saleroom in 1983 and was sold

s rare Ming jar fetched £16,000 at auction in
81, after being pieced together by a retired builder
o had found it in fragments in his yard.

Gospels of Henry the Lion was described as 'the
atest illuminated manuscript in private hands'
en it fetched a world-record price in 1983. Its
lden appearance in the saleroom ended fears that
ad been lost in the 1930s.

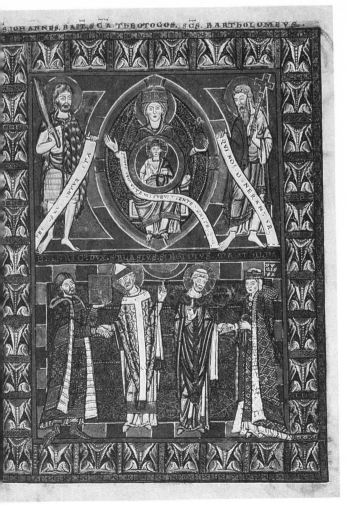

by its anonymous owners for £8,140,000, then a world-record auction price for a work of art. For their money, the book's German purchasers got one of the most important manuscripts of the Middle Ages: an edition of the four Gospels in Latin, adorned with more than 1,500 illuminated initials and thirty-one full-page pictures including portraits of Henry II and Thomas à Becket. An extra couple of curiosities were added when the book was rebound in the sixteenth century: in the centre of the cover is a dome of pure rock crystal, enclosing relics of two saints, Sigismund and Mark, tastefully wrapped. 'Perhaps a bit of one of the authors,' an onlooker remarked to a journalist.

Rebel without a gravestone

Film star James Dean's pink granite headstone went missing in 1983 from Fairmount, Indiana. It was found four years later, in May 1987, ignominiously dumped behind Fire Station Number 10 at Fort Wayne forty-five miles away.

The lost Cave of Cheddar

The Lost Cave of Cheddar has eluded potholers for centuries. Historian Henry of Huntingdon started the hunt back in the twelfth century by describing, in his *Historia Anglorum*, that although some underground explorers had 'traversed great spaces of land and rivers they could never come to the end'.

The known caves in Cheddar Gorge have already yielded a remarkable discovery. In 1990 archaeologists carrying out a survey for London's Natural History Museum announced that they had found the site of a long-forgotten museum in an overgrown grotto. The museum was established in 1914 by an eccentric to show off a collection of prehistoric artefacts and remains, but it never recovered from being vandalised. Soon it was engulfed by vegetation. The archaeologists' haul was a rich one: more than fifty flint tools were recovered, as well as pottery and bones dating from the Bronze Age.

No surrender?

There were red faces in Britain's Ministry of Defence when no one could find the official surrender document signed at the end of the Falklands War in 1982. It eventually turned up in an envelope containing a whole pile of unsorted papers brought back from the islands after the conflict and was promptly sent off to the safety of London's Imperial War Museum, where it is now on display.

The last relic of the Crystal Palace

Until 1985, it was thought that nothing remained of the greatest show-piece of the 1851 Great Exhibition, the Crystal Palace. The vast glass and iron edifice, which had stood in London's Hyde Park, was dismantled after the exhibition and re-erected at Sydenham where it was destroyed by fire in 1936. Nothing apparently survived the blaze. But unknown to the architectural historians, at least one relic of the Crystal Palace never made it to Sydenham. This was a cast-iron walkway which was built into the Royal Agricultural Hall in North London and was rediscovered when the building was being refurbished in 1985. Two clues convinced the experts: the first was that the plans of the Sydenham Crystal Palace show fewer walkways than its Hyde Park predecessor; the second was that the Prince's Gallery, as the Royal Agricultural Hall walkway is known, is in a completely different style to the rest of the building.

St Stephen's crown

Perhaps no object in history has been lost and found as often as the crown of St Stephen, Hungary's greatest treasure. Made sometime in the eleventh century, the crown is priceless: a circle of gold set with rubies, sapphires, pearls and an emerald. Yet:

- it was lost by a Bavarian prince in the fourteenth century and found buried in a bog.

- it was captured by the Turks in the sixteenth century.

- it was buried near Orsova, Austria, by rebels in the nineteenth century.

The Temple of Apollo at Didyma, Turkey. It was here that a keen-eyed German archaeologist solved the mystery of how the architects of the ancient world designed and built their masterpieces.

James Dean's gravestone restored to the star's plot in Fairmount, Indiana, after its four-year disappearance. Appropriately, the tragic heart-throb's middle initial stands for Byron.

- it went missing at the end of the Second World War and was found by the Americans concealed in an oil barrel which was, in turn, buried in a marsh – for the second time in its history.
- it disappeared again, and was eventually revealed to be in the possession of the United States Government, who finally, in 1978, returned it to its proper home in Budapest.

Ready to dig when you are . . .

In the early 1980s, plans were announced for one of the most curious archaeological excavations of all time. The idea was to uncover a gigantic Egyptian metropolis, the City of Rameses, containing a pharaoh's palace, a ceremonial avenue, rows of sphinxes and four huge statues of Rameses the Magnificent himself.

Oddly, these 'treasures of ancient Egypt' were not on the banks of the River Nile but in the sand dunes at Guadalupe, California, a small town north of Los Angeles. They formed part of a spectacular film set built, in 1923, by Cecil B. DeMille for the first version of his epic *The Ten Commandments*. When shooting had finished, DeMille decided that the cheapest way of disposing of the set would be simply to cover it with sand. According to his autobiography, the idea also amused him:

> If, a thousand years from now, archaeologists happen to dig beneath the sands of the Guadalupe, I hope they will not rush into print with the amazing news that Egyptian civilization, far from being confined to the Valley of the Nile, extended all the way to the Pacific Coast of North America.

Few people today, however, share DeMille's sense of the languorous march of the centuries – especially in Hollywood – and the set had been buried for a mere sixty years when it was located, and a campaign to save and restore one of the great curiosities of movie history was launched.

The stolen Stradivarius

Only a few hundred Stradivarius violins have survived since the heyday of Antonio Stradivari and his two sons in the seventeenth century, and the disappearance of one in modern times is nothing short of a disaster. Such was the reaction when one of the best of all the 'Master's' creations –

known as the 'Gibson' – was stolen from the Carnegie Hall dressing-room of Polish violinist Bronislaw Huberman in 1936.

It seemed to have vanished into thin air. The insurers paid out, and the loss was forgotten until 1985, when a New York violinist named Julian Altman was on his deathbed. As he lay there, he told his wife Marcelle to look carefully at his violin, a battered instrument which he had occasionally left in bars or on subway trains as he went about his business.

Inside the violin case, Marcelle found a yellowed bundle of press cuttings relating to the theft of the 'Gibson'. There was just time before his death for Altman to make a confession: he'd bought the Strad for $100 from the man who stole it on the day after the robbery. How he had come across the thief was never explained, and by no means everyone who heard the story believed that the encounter had ever taken place.

But this is a story with a happy ending. Altman died having unburdened himself of a guilty secret, the world of music was happy to reclaim one of the most exquisite violins ever made, and the instrument itself was sold on behalf of the original insurers for 'somewhat in excess of $1m', with Altman's widow benefiting from a quarter-million dollar reward for turning it in.

Hidden plans

Finally, a chance discovery which solved an age-old mystery.

In 1979, Lothar Haselberger took time out from a German Archaeological Institute study tour of the remains of the classical world to visit the Temple of Apollo at Didyma near Söke, Turkey.

The building impressed him, and he looked closely at the details of its construction: the fine fluted columns, the walls which seemed to have been designed to lean slightly inwards, and the courses of stone blocks which the stone masons had fitted together with uncanny precision. One thing, however, intrigued him above all else. Many of the temple's smoothest walls were covered in delicately traced lines, so faint that they could only be made out in certain light conditions.

What did they mean? Were they simply the result of the construction process or some unstudied type of classical graffito? Haselberger was determined to find an answer, and in doing so transformed a chance observation into an exciting archaeological study. For when he drew out the lines on paper, he found he was holding something for which archaeologists had been searching in vain for more than two centuries: a set of architectural drawings for one of the great buildings of antiquity.

The ancient Greeks wrote a greal deal about the philosophy of architecture and the magnificence of their surviving buildings is ample testimony to their engineering and construction skills. Their working plans, however, were thought to have perished with them.

At Didyma, Haselberger found 'blueprints' which covered hundreds of square metres: every smooth surface seems to have been used and the architectural features were drawn full size. The builders apparently covered their stone 'drawing boards' with a red pigment before precisely engraving the lines with a metal gouge. Traces of the pigment can still be seen. Even the plans of the foundations and early stages of the temple have come to light.

Why did the plans of the temple at Didyma survive when those other buildings dating from the same era seem to have disappeared? Haselberger offers an intriguing theory. The temple was never finished. If it had been, the stone on which the 'blueprints' were carved would have been polished, wiping out all trace of the lines. That incising the working drawings on the building itself was a widely practised technique has been confirmed by subsequent discoveries at other sites. In hindsight, perhaps, the working drawings should not have taken so long to find, for, as Haselberger points out, artisans of later generations used similar techniques: the builders of many of Europe's great Gothic cathedrals, like York Minster, for example, carved their plans on the 'site' itself. A reminder that the answers to many mysteries may lie, waiting to be found, right under our noses.

4

Crazy competitions

If there's one place on earth that specialises in crazy competitions and record-breaking curiosities, it's the town of Pepinster in Belgium. Once a year, its citizens dedicate a weekend to weird championships. In 1987, for example, a tough-guy called Jacques took less than an hour to blow up and burst forty hot-water bottles and another macho character called Giovanni managed to balance a car on a see-saw for an hour and ten seconds. Nearby stood the world's largest deckchair, and the world's biggest clothespeg, and the town museum proudly exhibited a monster croissant containing eighty pounds of butter. In fact, so many visitors cram into the place to watch the feats and the fun, that Pepinster is in danger of setting another, less desirable record – for traffic jams.

Pepinster has at least one European rival in the record-breaking stakes – the village of Aubigny in France. And the French probably win the prize for the saddest championships of all, the Snail Grand Prix held in Alsace. Ten snails, named after leading French football teams race on wooden tracks which have been soaked with water to encourage them. The winner gets a kiss from the reigning Miss Escargot, but then, for the snails, the celebrations come to an abrupt and miserable end, for the winner and his rivals are consigned to the pot and served up, dripping with garlic butter, to the hungry spectators.

While every country does its best to stage weird and wonderful championships, there is, as always, no beating the United States for the sheer variety and outrageous inventiveness behind its competitions and special days. So our advice to anyone who combines curiosity with competitiveness is – Go West and sample some of these crazy competitions.

At Seeley Lake, Montana, they hold an annual **Magathon**, sponsored of course by **WORM** (the World Organization of Racing Maggots). Time-

A winner at the New Jersey Championship Tomato Weigh-In, the self-styled 'America's No. 1 Big Tomato Contest.'

competitor parades his 'feathered boy' at the International Chicken ing Meet at Rio Grande, Ohio.

trials, grudge matches and the climactic 'dash-for-the-cash' final are run – or squirmed – over a foot-long six-lane course at Barney's Bar and Café.

At Guerneville, north of San Francisco, California, the Banana Slug Festival is a kind of Olympics for the 10-inch long slimy gastropods which breed in the local redwood groves. The slugs slither sedately around a racetrack, but this is far less arduous than the task facing the judges of the **banana slug recipe contest**. A recent entry by a top chef was described by a visiting reporter as a 'gelatinous rainbow of beets, asparagus, artichokes and chunks of suspended slugs, garnished with pansies and flowering kale'.

Burlington, Wisconsin, boasts a Liars Club which organises the **World Lying Championships**. The 1986 winner was a certain Mr Clarence H. Klott of Herman, Missouri. More than 300 fibbers fought it out, but Clarence floored 'em with this whopper, 'A new landowner asked an elderly neighbour if it ever rained there. His reply, "Well, you read in the Bible about 40 days and 40 nights of rain. Well, that time we got a quarter of an inch."'

Everyone corpses at the sight of the annual Goodwater, Alabama, **Casket Race**, in which competitors have to act as pall-bearers and manœuvre a coffin over a course littered with obstacles, including old tyres, a mud pit and a pile of sawdust. Even the 'cadaver' competes: he or she has to carry a cup of water all the way without spilling a drop.

Big rewards were on offer in 1984 for the first USA's **Ugliest College Man Contest** held in Indiana, Pennsylvania. The prize most keenly competed for was $50 worth of plastic surgery.

There's a chance to see double at two American events: the annual **Mother-Daughter Look-Alike Contest**, held at Pomona, California, and the **Twins Festival** at – surprise, surprise – Twinsburg, Ohio.

At Twin Lakes, Colorado, a sure aim is essential for success in the yearly **Tomato Wars**. In 1983, a team of Texans de-splat-ched the home team by bombing them with tomato juice from a plane, but the Coloradoans got their own back in 1984 with a volley of messy missiles. A cunning tomato warrior could ensure victory with a quick trip to Eatontown, New Jersey, home of the **New Jersey Championship Tomato Weigh-in**. One recent winner tipped the scales at 4.034 pounds, and measured $22\frac{3}{4}$ inches.

At Pardeeville, Wisconsin, competitors have to spit with polish to win the annual **Watermelon Seed Spitting Contest**. The record's nothing less than a spit supreme at 48 ft 2 ins. And while we're on the subject, let's not forget the **Tobacco Spitting Contest** at the Wood County Fair in Virginia. You won't be surprised to hear that the rules are vaguely disgusting: competitors stand at the end of a 21 foot-long board. If they miss it, or the spit is smaller than an American quarter coin when it lands, the competitor is disqualified. In fact, there are plenty of competitions for lovers of the unsavoury, not least the **World Championship Cow Chip Contest**. 'Cow Chip' is American for cowpat, and the winner of the 1985 contest at Beaver, Oklahoma, managed to sling one more than 177 feet.

Birds and animals compete in many bizarre American contests. There's big money on offer at the **Great American Duck Race** in Deming, New Mexico: the purse recently was $7,500. And after the quack-pot contest, winners and losers can unwind at the Duck Ball. At the **Calaveras County Fair and Jumping Frog Jubilee** in Angels Camp, California, one nimble little fellow failed to jump far enough to win his heat of the **International Frog Finals** – the record stands at over 20 ft – but he did hop right into the headlines when a photographer caught him (and his owner) in full flight. And everything they say about beauty contests was confirmed at the **All-American Glamour Kitty Contest** in Bal Harbour, Florida, in 1983. It is said that when the lovely Leona took the prize, cries of 'Miaow, miaow' filled the air, and losers threatened to scratch each other's eyes out. Chickens – or their owners – seem to be particularly competitive. They meet every year on Bob Evans's farm at Rio Grande, Ohio, for the **International Chicken Flying Meet**, and at Rogue River, Oregon, there's the **Oregon Rooster Crowing Contest**, in which the prize is awarded to the cock which crows most within a thirty-minute time limit. In 1986 an **Old-Time Costume Poultry Contest** was back at the Kentucky State Fair by popular demand. The idea, as you'll have guessed, is to parade a chicken or duck in fancy dress. Among the birds, an invitation to take part in the **World's Chicken Pluckin' Contest** at Spring Hill, Florida, is presumably not highly prized. One competition where you will not come across a bird of any kind is the **Nut Tree Scarecrow Contest** at Vacaville, California.

In Virginia, wild ponies swim from Assateague Island across the Assateague Channel to Chincoteague in the annual **Pony Swim**, while Dillon, Colorado, a tiny settlement of some three hundred inhabitants, is the mecca of owners of burros – the donkeys used by old-style American miners. The town holds an annual **Lake Dillon Burro Race** along a seven-mile mountain trail. Even more exotic contests feature on the bill at the **Camel Races** at Virginia City, Nevada, while no upwardly mobile canine competitor would dream of missing one of the local or state heats of the **Gaines Ashley Whippet Invitational for Frisbee-Catching Dogs**. And if you want to get rid of an unsuccessful pet, you could do worse than see how your sales technique compares with the spiel of rival entrants to the **World Livestock Auctioneer Championship**. In 1985, more than a hundred auctioneers made their way to Humeston, Iowa, to take part.

If they can't get to grips with the gavel, people with loud voices can try

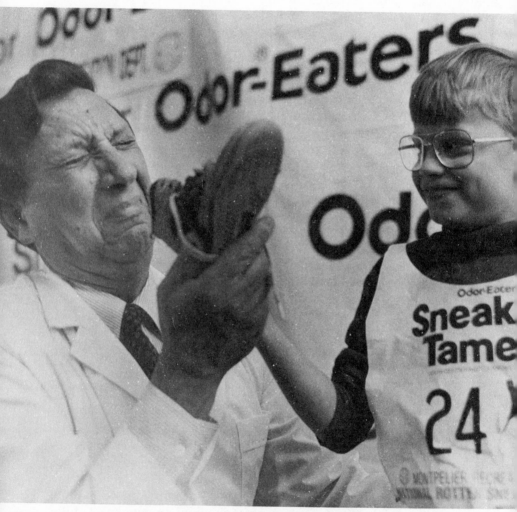

Phew, what a stinker! Judge Dr Herbert Lapidus bravely samples a whiff of 8-year-old Robert Scruton's smelly training shoe, winner of the American Rotten Sneaker Contest.

North Carolina's **National Hollerin' Contest** at Spivey's Corner. The **Turkey-Calling Contest** is held around Thanksgiving in Arkansas. The venue? Yellville, of course.

Far less salubrious is the **American Rotten Sneakers Contest**. Traditionally held in Montpelier, Vermont, the contest became a world-wide event from 1989. However, foreigners face considerable competition if the standards set by the thirteen preceding contests are anything to go by. In 1988, the winner was an eight-year-old schoolboy who had been preparing his particularly nauseating Nikes for no less than two years! Almost as stomach-churning is the **Great American Roach-Off**, described as 'a coast-to-coast quest for the state with the biggest bugs'. The cockroaches that make the final come in alarming sizes: a recent $1,000 prizewinner, found on the beach at Hallandale, Florida, was a grotesque 2.08 inches long. The brute was displayed at the Smithsonian Institution, Washington D.C., for a year. Clute, Texas, is a place where they thriftily make use of the town's 'only natural resource'. Hence the **Great Texas Mosquito Festival**. Highlights include a beauty contest where the winner gets to call herself Ms Quito.

Eating competitions of all types abound, but the strongest stomachs of all are to be found at the **World Championship Worm Cook-Off** in Ontario, California. Recipes are enthusiastically exchanged. Rather more attractive is the annual **Egg Cream Drinking Contest** in which a recent winner knocked back an egg cream (made from seltzer, milk and chocolate syrup) in one two-second glutinous gulp. At the **Brussels Sprout Harvest Festival** at Santa Cruz, California, in 1987, eating the green goodies (even though some were coated in chocolate) took second place to putting them. In a contest that gave a new meaning to the term 'golfing greens,' the prize was a trip to Brussels, Belgium – of course.

And if you prefer slightly less exotic tasks, there's the annual Philadelphia **Bedmaking Championships**, where points are won or lost for hospital corners and the amount of sheet folded over at the top. Even better, for the contestants, must be the **Tropical Blend Power Lounging Competition**. To win a $500 prize, all they had to do at the 1987 event was to create an ideal suntanning environment on a ten-foot section of beach at Pacific Palisades, California.

As you make your bed so you must lie. Which brings us to the **Pegleg Liars Contest** in Borrego Springs, California. Each competitor has to tell a mendacious tale about a gentleman called Pegleg who apparently set standards in fibbing in the 1930s when he claimed there was gold by the ton in the Santa Rosa Mountains.

In America, sporting prowess of every type is catered for. At Mount Vernon, Washington, a few sweet-toothed daredevils are allowed to compete in the **Annual Jell-O Jump** where they have to plunge into a vat of cherry jelly. Strangest of all the events at the **World Eskimo Indian Olympics** in Fairbanks, Alaska, is the ear-pulling contest. Competitors pull at strings attached to each other's lobes until one gives up. Almost as uncomfortable – even to contemplate – is the contest to see who can go furthest with an 18-pound weight dangling from one earlobe. Even the less obviously athletic can let off steam in the **Short Fat Guys Road Race** at Redmond, Oregon.

Charities have found that there's nothing like a bizarre event for attracting attention to their cause and for raising cash. Competitors in the annual **World Heavyweight Ski Championships** held at Sugarloaf Mountain, Maine, have to pay an entry fee of a few cents for every pound they weigh. Among the other rules: skiers must tip the scales at at least 250 lbs. Many veritable human avalanches weigh far more, but the mountain is still standing.

Not every American heart, however, burns with competitive zeal. At Durham, New Hampshire, a few dozen people of Scandinavian descent wander into town for the annual **Leif Ericson Celebration Parade**, held each October to commemorate the man who, according to the Icelandic sagas, may have discovered America by mistake – due to a navigation error – almost 500 years before Columbus. It's difficult to stray from today's commemorative route: it runs from the Durham Launder Center laundromat to Young's Restaurant – next door!

In towns where the greatest excitement lies in the weekly visit to the supermarket, shoppers can give their competitive spirits free rein by practising for the **All-American Paper Grocery Sack Pack-Offs**. The rules are strict – for example, breakable goods must be placed at the top and bags must balance properly – but the prizes are worthwhile. These include the Charles Stilwell Award (he invented a bag machine in 1883) and trips to Pack-Offs in New York City and Los Angeles.

If literature is your bag, then the competition to enter is the **International Imitation Hemingway Competition** organised by Harry's Bar and American Grill in Los Angeles, a replica of 'Papa's' favourite Italian hideaway. Gems from recent winners include: 'The man, whose name was nondescript, unslung his Miaquina, and placed it on the bar top, gently, as if it was asleep and he wished it not to wake. It was his favourite machine gun. They had been together for years.' Another fine entry read: "She is truly one of magnificent spirit," thought Ricardo, as the American woman called Louise broke a bottle of Campari over his head.'

Finally, probably the weirdest contest of all, the **International Worm Fiddling Contest** at Caryville, Florida. No, it's not a competition for wriggling musical prodigies. Competitors simply drive a wooden stake into the

Not a leg to stand on. Only the tallest stories and most formidable fibs stand a chance in the Pegleg Liars Contest in Borrego Springs, California.

earth and hit it with something heavy – a technique known as 'fiddling'. All being well, the worms in the ground around the stake pop up and have a look around.

5

Aliens in our midst

In November 1987 the authorities in East Anglia in England pronounced the coypu extinct. The coypu is a large rat-like creature, up to three feet long with thick fur. Its end was greeted with celebration. A spokesman said, 'It has taken us a quarter of a century to get rid of it. It is perfectly all right in its own country, South America, but here it has been an absolute menace, attacking crops and damaging river banks. It's good riddance.'

The coypu, which escaped, like mink, from fur farms in the 1930s, was one of many strange species which are loose in Britain. Others include hamsters in North London, wallabies in Derbyshire and Chinese muntjac deer and parakeets in the South of England.

Strange creatures sometimes surface in road accidents. An Indian nilgai antelope jumped over a hedge in Kent in 1980 and killed two people in a car. A wild boar was run over and killed on a forestry road in Nairn in Scotland in 1976. It was nearly a century since the last wild boar had been heard of in Britain. No one could account for the Scottish creature's origin. In April 1988, a leopard cat was shot by a farmer at Widecombe in the Moor on Dartmoor, Devon. Again, how it got there was never explained.

In 1980, three separate people called the police to say they had seen a crocodile crossing the M55 motorway at Preston in Lancashire. On another occasion, a twelve-year-old girl found a dead crocodile behind her house in Caerphilly in Wales. She carted the five-foot-long creature to school. Health officials took it away. What seemed to be a crocodile was squashed by a car in Dulwich, London, in 1972.

In 1981, some fishermen from Peterhead, Aberdeenshire, came across a dead elephant floating in the sea off the Scottish coast.

6

Jumped-up creatures

The human high-jump record may be approaching eight feet, but other creatures seem to be a lot better at defying gravity.

In 1985 British television reporter David Lomax was sailing his yacht *Cloud Walker* across the Atlantic from Grand Canary to Antigua when he woke up to find that a giant squid had leaped ten feet out of the water and caught itself in the rigging. He was the first-known sailor to have actually trapped a squid in flight. The dreaded beasts – the largest of which, with their fearful beaks and suckers, have been known to attack even the huge sperm whale – have great mantle fins which seem to act as wings when they 'jet' themselves into the air. Some squid have been observed to travel more than fifty yards through the air before planing down into the water again.

On land, there are extraordinary feats of jumping by small creatures – not least the flea! But among the great animals there can be few to match the tiger. Even the classic ruse of climbing a tree seems to offer no refuge. Brigadier W. M. T. Magan of Tonbridge, Kent, reported that he had been out in the Indian jungle when he had seen tiger claw-marks on a tree. With his Indian *shikari* (sporting guide), the Brigadier measured the height of the scratches. They were over seventeen feet.

'We supposed the tiger had been trying to catch a monkey,' he wrote. 'And it may have succeeded!'

7

Bighead!

Many years ago now, we both worked on a regional television news programme which, in addition to the main events of the day, used to feature weird and wonderful stories from the huge area of northern Britain served by our television station. Many details of the first programme we made have, fortunately, faded from our memories – it was *not* a success. But we do remember one story with some affection. It came from a letter in the weekly *New Statesman*. A woman from Sheffield wrote to say that her husband had an enormous head, 26 inches in circumference.

> We think, [she added] that he must surely hold another record – that of being the only serviceman in the last war to go through his basic training without headgear. On the occasion of my weekend visits to him, a favourite occupation was NCO baiting. We would see, with pleasure, one of them advancing upon us with a baleful glint in his eye, only to gape incredulously when told, 'Sorry, chum, waiting for size 8!' When the forage cap and steel helmet eventually arrived, they were, as the French would say, *formidable*.

The star of our film certainly did have an impressive head, but it didn't of course compare with the *really* big bonces that sculptors have created throughout the world.

The Mount Rushmore sculptures nearing completion in 1941. To carve the rock, design Gutzon Borglum (below) and his fellow workers had to dangle from bosuns' chairs.

Granite grandees

The huge faces carved on the side of Mount Rushmore in the Black Hills of South Dakota are a spectacular tribute to four US Presidents: Washington, Jefferson, Lincoln and Theodore Roosevelt.

The first scheme, put forward in the 1920s and designed to attract tourists to the area, was to commission sculptures of famous figures from the days of the Wild West. Designer Gutzon Borglum, however, proposed the more grandiose plan of portraying the four Presidents, and work began in 1927. Fourteen years, a million dollars and countless dynamite blasts later, the giant sculpture was completed. Almost half a million tons of rock had been removed and countless man-hours taken up in carving the detail of the faces, each of which is 60 feet high.

But perhaps the most curious thing about Mount Rushmore is how it got its name. Instead of being named after some historical bigwig, it bears the name of an obscure lawyer. According to the story, a gold miner was riding past the mountain with his attorney, whose name was Rushmore. 'What's the name of that mountain?' asked the legal-eagle. 'Why Mount Rushmore, of course,' the cheeky miner replied. The name stuck, and in 1930 the mountain was officially given its name.

Rushmore's rival

Just sixteen miles from Mount Rushmore, a new giant head is being chipped from the rock of another Black Hills peak, Thunderhead Mountain. This time it does commemorate one of the characters of the Old West passed over at Mount Rushmore in favour of the Presidents. Sculptor Korczak Ziolkowski was working on the Rushmore memorial when a Sioux chief told him that his tribe had always dreamed that an effigy of Crazy Horse, the celebrated hero of Custer's Last Stand in 1876, would be carved from a mountainside overlooking the ancient Indian hunting-grounds.

Ziolkowski began work in 1948. He had less than $150 in his pocket and only a tent to live in, but he was a man obsessed. He believed that by sculpting Crazy Horse – not just his head, by the way, but the Chief's trusty steed too – he would atone for the injustices meted out to the Indians during the colonisation of America.

But by the time Ziolkowski died in 1982, the great statue was very far from finished, despite the fact that he had hacked more than seven million tons of rock from the face of the 6,700 foot mountain. He had conceived the work on a truly gigantic scale – even drawing the outlines took more than 170 gallons of white paint. The sculpture, when and if it is finally completed by Ziolkowski's wife and ten children, will be 641 feet long and 563 feet high. 4,000 people at once will be able to stand on Crazy Horse's outstretched arm and each of his nostrils will be large enough to encompass a five-roomed house.

Monumental controversy

Ferdinand Marcos, the late President of the Philippines, was never shy of borrowing ideas from the Americans. He had this 'mini-Rushmore' built on a golf course at Pugo village, 120 miles north of Manila. Construction work was halted from time to time by the recurring financial crises that led to his undoing, but eventually the 50 foot effigy, showing a smiling dictator, complete with slicked-back hair and natty shirt, was finished – just in time to see him deposed and sent into exile.

After the revolution, there were calls to blow up the gigantic bust – the loudest from the tribes whose land had been taken for the site. But the new government had a better idea: they decided to keep it, as a symbol of repression and a reminder of the bad old days.

Talking Turkey

In 1851 a group of mapmakers made a curious discovery in the Ankar mountains of Turkey. They noticed that one peak, Nemrut Dag, had an artificial summit. When they reached it, they saw why. For according to inscriptions found there, the place was a temple, built in the first century BC by King Antiochus I of the kingdom of Commagene in honour of 'all the gods'. Its most striking feature: huge heads of Antiochus himself and of Zeus, Tyche, Heracles and Apollo, flanked by eagles and lions. The heads are about 30 feet high, and most still lie where they fell after being toppled from their platforms by an earthquake. Yet even in its ruined state, Nemrut Dag is unforgettable. Wrote one recent visitor, 'the silent monumentality of these stones, looking out over serried ranks of peaks marking the unofficial start of Kurdistan, is profound and moving.' However, Edward Mace, Travel Editor of the London *Observer*, described Nemrut Dag in rather less reverential terms in 1985:

notorious Ferdinand Marcos, President of the Philippines, had this ego-boosting 'mini-Rushmore' of self constructed outside Manila. It is as high as a four-storey house.

The statues brood over the ruins of the palace with an air of malign discontent, the epitome of the misuse of power. At least, their giant bodies do. Their enormous heads, which weigh tons, are strewed all over like feathers. Nemrut Dag is convincing evidence that man has always been as mad as a hatter.

8

Out of the frame

The pride of St John's Cathedral in Valletta, Malta, is a huge painting by Caravaggio of St Jerome contemplating a skull. One Saturday in 1984, as the warden was ushering out the last visitors, he glanced up at the wall. There was nothing there. Thieves had calmly removed the painting from the wall and walked out with it.

Three years later, the picture was found folded up and badly creased in a house in Valletta. The police arrested two local men and an Italian shoe manufacturer.

The same year, five gunmen walked into the Marmottan Museum in Paris. They selected nine of the world's most famous Impressionist paintings, including Monet's *Impression of Sunrise*, took them outside to a waiting car, and drove off with the boot still open. The paintings had a market value of £50 million or more. Yet they are so well known that they are unsaleable in any public sense. In late 1987 the police raided a house in Japan after a tip-off that the paintings were there, but they were not returned until December 1990, from a hiding-place in Corsica.

The business of art theft is a colossal and mysterious enterprise, with all sorts of motives. Why bother to fold up the Caravaggio in a corner for three years?

Rembrandt's portrait of Jacob van Gheyn, probably the most stolen picture in the world. When not forcibly detained elsewhere, it can be found in London's Dulwich Picture Gallery.

Take your pix

Perhaps there really is a super-rich and insane collector of Impressionist pictures. Apart from the nine Monets, Renoirs, Morisots etc. stolen in Paris, there are another eighteen still missing since 1982 from the Montreal Museum of Fine Arts. Again gunmen walked in, in broad daylight, picked up a Delacroix, a Corot and a Millet, as well as a Rembrandt and a Rubens for good measure, and drove away.

Crimes on commission

Art robberies are often thought to have been commissioned. Two Raphaels, two Tintorettos and two Tiepolos were stolen from the Budapest Museum in Hungary in 1983. They were recovered three months later and a Greek olive-oil manufacturer was arrested and charged with commissioning the theft. The charges were later dropped, though the thieves, three Italians and two Hungarians, were convicted.

Miraculous recoveries

At any one time there are at least 50,000 missing works of art of sufficient value to be on Interpol's lists, their saleroom worth running into literally billions of pounds. On past performance, less than a quarter of them will be recovered.

But they do turn up. Eleven Impressionist paintings stolen in Florida in 1981 were found on a rubbish dump 1,000 miles north in Boston in 1982. A Renoir turned up in a flat in Manhattan and an El Greco was spotted in the lumber of a London police station's lost property vault.

Now you see it . . .

The most stolen object in the world is probably the nicely portable portrait of Jacob van Gheyn by Rembrandt in the Dulwich Picture Gallery, London. It was stolen and recovered in 1967, 1973 and 1981. In 1983 thieves got in through a skylight and removed it for a fourth time. It was found again in 1986 in the thieves' favourite deposit – a railway left-luggage office in Münster, Germany. The parcel containing the picture had been there for so long that the staff were apparently on the point of throwing it away when the police arrived.

Paintings are often taken for ransom. A lorry driver stole Goya's portrait of the Duke of Wellington from the National Gallery in London, in order, he said, to force the government to give free television licences to old-age pensioners. He subsequently left it four years later, in 1965, in the left-luggage office at Birmingham New Street station.

In 1986 three men and two women stole Picasso's *Woman in Tears* from the Victoria State Art Gallery in Australia. They threatened to burn it if the government did not increase its grant to the arts and agree to set up two $5,000 annual prizes for young painters.

Art thieves can also be extraordinarily enterprising. A Renoir was simply hooked with some kind of fishing rod through the door of Wildenstein's gallery in London in 1987, thereby avoiding setting off the burglar alarms.

Around the globe, lost, stolen or strayed, there are probably more missing masterpieces than there are on all the walls of all the world's galleries.

9

Moving stories

In 1981, an extraordinary photograph was included in a London exhibition of the work of Richard and Sally Greenhill. It shows a strange sight – to British eyes. A complete house on the back of a lorry, parked in a field near Stapleton, Nebraska. There are still many Americans, particularly those who live in the old country homesteading areas, who find the idea of *really* moving house – not just flinging possessions into a tea chest and a removal van, but transporting a complete building to another site – unremarkable. The houses involved are usually designed to be moved, but increasingly, throughout the world, more solid buildings are 'travelling' – for all kinds of reasons.

In Aberdeen, Scotland, for example, a granite building on the corner of King Street was dismantled stone by stone and shifted a few yards to make room for a dual-carriageway. It is now the Consumer Advice Centre. Many museums contain buildings rescued from the demolition squads. Aarhus, Denmark, boasts one such new 'old town', and Greenfield Village at Deerborn, Michigan, USA, features Edison's laboratories, the birthplace of the Wright brothers and the home of Edgar Allan Poe among its reconstructed glories.

Increasingly, few American movers allow the size of a building to get in their way. In April 1985 the Fairmount Hotel was rolled through San Antonio, Texas, to a site four blocks from where it was originally erected in 1906. The move was quite an operation, for the hotel weighed no less than 3.2 million pounds and had to be transported on a framework of steel beams resting on thirty-six hydraulic dollies. And the reason for the move, which cost a million dollars? A more profitable use had been found for the hotel's original site – as a shopping mall.

The British, who have an abundance of beautiful ancient churches,

ABOVE Moving house American-style. This fundamental form of removals is practised throughout the United States. Richard and Sally Greenhill captured this homestead *en route* through Nebraska.

BELOW In San Antonio, Texas, the venerable Fairmount Hotel turns a city corner on the second day o four-day move to a new site. The 1,650 ton structure was the heaviest ever moved whole on wheels.

have found overseas buyers for redundant ecclesiastical buildings, despite the fact that they cannot be moved in one piece and have to be taken down stone by stone and later reassembled. At Fulton, Missouri, for example, a transplanted church stands, somewhat bizarrely, as a memorial to a speech made there by Sir Winston Churchill. It was the one in which he coined the phrase 'the iron curtain'.

Occasionally, old buildings are imported *into* Britain. One of the most celebrated is the Norwegian barn which was brought to Elstree, Hertfordshire, in 1903 by an English couple who had spotted it while on holiday in Norway and just had to have it. Apart from its odd origins, the barn's chief claim to fame is that it was the house from which Sophia Loren was robbed of her jewellery while making *The Millionairess* at the nearby film studios.

Parts of buildings have also been moved lock, stock and barrel. For example, the Bridge Inn Toby Hotel at Walshford, Yorkshire, on one of Britain's oldest and busiest roads, the A1, contains a dining room once used by Lord Byron on his honeymoon at Halnaby Hall, Durham. It's now a private function suite. One of Britain's finest art museums, the Burrell Collection in Glasgow, Scotland, includes the dining room, drawing room and hall from its founder's home, Hutton Castle, near Berwick-on-Tweed on the English-Scottish border. And the rooms hadn't even originated there: they came from a house called Harrington Hall – in Lincolnshire.

Panelling from the old offices of *The Times* in Printing House Square, London, is now in Berlin. The wood was bought by German press tycoon Axel Springer when *The Times* building was rebuilt in 1962 and installed in a club for foreign journalists atop a Berlin skyscraper. And a sizeable chunk of the old Opera House from Dunfermline, Scotland, lives on, despite the fact that the original building was demolished in 1981. The theatre's fine plasterwork was carefully kept and later shipped to Sarasota, Florida, to adorn a new performing arts centre.

The Princess of Wales was presented with an old window which would otherwise have been thrown out when her Norfolk birthplace, Park House near Sandringham, was being converted into an hotel for the disabled. The window had been near the telephone and was the place where the Spencer family used to scrawl useful telephone numbers. These apparently included the Princess's school, local tradesmen and those well-known Norfolk telephonists 'Old Mother Riley' and 'Pontius Pilate'!

Here are some other remarkable 'transplants'.

A long way from the
Thames. It took forty
men twenty-three
months to reassembl
all the 10,276 granit
blocks of London Brid
after its transatlantic
journey to Lake
Havasu, Arizona.

Sam Krogstad, the m
who got the US Mail
do his removals for
him. He sent a whole
harbour, block by blo
and neatly labelled,
through the post.

An Eiffel in New Orleans

Le Restaurant de la Tour Eiffel in St Charles Avenue, New Orleans in the United States, isn't merely named after the great Parisian landmark: it was actually part of it. The elegant eatery was once the Eiffel Tower's second-level restaurant, but it had to be dismantled in 1981, when engineers decided that the tower was so overloaded with structures that the whole thing was in danger of sagging. So the restaurant was carefully dismantled into thousands of pieces and packed into a crate, 40 feet long. Every section was labelled. The giant 'construction kit' was then sent by boat to New York (there were legal restraints about opening a grounded Eiffel tower restaurant in France), and it finally reached its owners, who lavished some $3 million on its purchase and refurbishment, via the New Orleans train.

Old England gone west

As we have seen, Americans take any opportunity to buy up the redundant landmarks of old England. In fact, the only thing they seem reluctant to import is the country's most distinctive and talked-about feature, its weather. So there is no authentic fog shrouding London Bridge, now at Lake Havasu City, Arizona, after being bought in 1975 by oilman Robert McCollough for £1,250,000. It came in 10,000 pieces and cost several million dollars more to reassemble.

No rest for mon repos

Bert Hinkler may not be a household name in England, but he certainly is in the town of Bundaberg in Queensland, Australia. In fact, they have re-erected his household as a memorial to him. It is called 'Mon Repos', and the humble dwelling originally stood in the English city of Southampton.

The reason for the Bundabergers' keenness to commemorate Bert? Well, he was their most famous son, a pioneer aviator who flew solo to Australia in 1928, and they felt that dismantling 'Mon Repos' brick by brick and transporting it to Australia was the best way of commemorating their local hero and of celebrating the town's bi-centenary at the same time.

The weirdest, the wildest, the cheapest

Here are a few candidates for the title of weirdest move of all.

In 1987, a supermarket company contributed £25,000 towards the removal – to a site four miles away – of an English meadow. The firm's plans to build on the field at Monkspath, Solihull, in the West Midlands, had alarmed conservationists, for it was the home of rare and picturesquely named wildflowers, including the Dyer's Greenweed, the Sneezewort and the Heath Spotted Orchid. There was only one way of keeping everybody happy – to move the whole meadow. And that is exactly what a team of ecologists did, with the help of machines which cut it into easily transported blocks.

In 1990 an entire wood at Bourton on the Dorset-Somerset border was moved to save it from destruction by motorway builders. It cost £15 million to transport the coppice of alder and hazel trees a few hundred yards to safety.

Perhaps even more remarkable is the method used by Mrs Lana Scott to move her goods and chattels from Alaska to Waukee, Iowa. Appalled by the cost of a conventional removal van, she simply sent all her possessions to her address by parcel post – in 800 parcels.

In 1988, Sam Krogstad, a construction supplier in Anchorage, Alaska, went one better: he sent a whole harbour through the mail to Wainwright some 700 miles to the north. Although the stamps cost him about $45,000 ($4.33 for each of the 6,000 concrete blocks and $4.27 for each of the 4,600 bags of cement supplied), Mr Krogstad saved a fortune on conventional shipping bills. And since each parcel was within the legal weight limits, the Postal Service had no option but to accept the consignments and deliver them.

10

Return from the dead

Around the world, animals thought to be extinct are constantly turning up. Most famous of all 'returns from the dead' is that of the **coelacanth**, a fish thought to have been extinct for sixty million years – until 1938 when it was found to be alive and well and swimming happily about in the sea of south-east Africa.

Even Indo-China, battered by fifty years of war and despoliation has its success stories. In 1982, a small herd of five **koupreys** was spotted on the borders of Thailand and Cambodia. The kouprey is the wild forest ox, looking intriguingly like the cattle which early man drew on the cave walls of Lascaux and Altamira. It had been thought to be extinct for at least thirty years.

Further south in Sarawak, 1986 saw the discovery of a group of **woolly rhinos** in a remote valley. They too had been thought extinct for forty years.

Sometimes tenacity in the search for supposedly extinct species pays off – in the oddest circumstances. The hunt for **Jerdon's Courser**, an Indian bird seen only three times after its discovery in 1848 and not at all in this century, ended one night in 1986 when a trapper helping a Bombay History Society expedition chanced to pick up a bird mesmerised by the light from his torch. It was a Jerdon's courser. This was a remarkable ending to a search for which few had predicted success, although for sheer amazing coincidence nothing can beat the moment when another supposedly extinct bird called **Macgillivray's petrel** 'returned from the dead'. It landed right on the head of the person who was hunting it!

Yet another Lazarus-like comeback was reported in October 1990. This was the **Australian Night Parrot**, *Geopsittacus Occidentalis*, which no one had spotted since 1912. However, the ornithologist who made the

Woolly rhinos like this were thought to have become museum pieces, but a group turned up alive and well and far from extinct in Sarawak in 1986.

remarkable discovery had mixed feelings. The specimen was lying by the roadside, probably after being hit by a car, and though not extinct was dead.

11

Lost villages

America is full of ghost towns where settlers stopped and built at the call of some sudden chance of fortune – gold, cattle, oil – and then moved on, as the seam ended or the whim passed.

In the confines of Britain's settled and sedate society, ghost towns, lost villages, abandoned settlements, are unexpected. Yet there are hundreds of lost settlements in the British Isles, some like **Semerwater** in Yorkshire, now beneath a lake, and whole towns on the East Coast like **Dunwich** (see page 171) which vanished beneath the sea. But many remain as eerie memorials to generations who eventually found the struggle too much and loaded their wagons and stole away.

Walk across the lonely wolds south of Malton in Yorkshire, and suddenly above a ridge appears a church spire. Only close at hand does the landscape abruptly dip to reveal a roofless but quite intact church. There is a graveyard, still walled against the moorland sheep and cattle, and a cottage. All around are ruins and the outlines of abandoned houses, barns and schools. This is **Wharram Percy**, a large and once prosperous medieval village, now entirely deserted after probably thousands of years of habitation, back to Roman times at least. No one knows whether it was the Black Death, landlords' enclosures, or some nameless disaster which sounded the knell of Wharram Percy.

But ghost towns are not all ancient. **Polphail** in Argyllshire, Scotland, was built in 1976 for workers constructing the North Sea oil platforms. By the time it was ready, the work had gone away. No one came to live in Polphail.

Cheesewring in Cornwall suffered a similar fate in the 1950s when the local quarry finally closed.

But the most evocative of the lost villages of Britain are in the Highlands and Islands of Scotland. **St Kilda**, most westerly of the islands, was abandoned as a communal act of despair when the last thirty-six islanders begged the navy to take them away, and were put aboard HMS *Harebell*, leaving the schoolhouse, the church, the factor's house and the sixteen cottages of the village street.

Of all the deserted islands, **Samson** in the Scillies is perhaps the most romantic. During the Napoleonic Wars the islanders woke one morning to find a French barque becalmed in the Sound beside Samson Island. With remarkable bravado, nineteen of the young men of the island rowed out in their boats and stormed aboard the Frenchman, capturing it and its crew of ten. Triumphantly they took the ship, first to St Mary's, and then set sail for Devonport to claim the money for their prize. Sadly the ship ran onto the Wolf Rock and was lost with all hands, Frenchmen and Englishmen and prize money too.

The women, children and old men were left bereft on Samson. For forty years they kept up an increasingly poverty-stricken life before they were finally taken off to St Mary's. Today the island is abandoned, but the signs of the old fields and houses can still be detected.

12

The Seven Wonders of the World

Before we tell you what remains of the Seven Wonders of the Ancient World, ask yourself this question: what *were* the Seven Wonders? The Pyramids of Egypt, of course, and the Hanging Gardens of Babylon. But can you name the other five?

In ancient times there wasn't, in fact, a definitive list. Even Philon of Byzantium and Antipatros of Sidon, the writers usually credited with first describing the Wonders, disagreed. But today there is no argument. The remaining five were the Statue of Zeus at Olympia, the Mausoleum at Halicarnassus, the Pharos Lighthouse off Alexandria, the Colossus of Rhodes and the Temple of Diana at Ephesus. All were within travelling distance of Greece, Egypt or Asia Minor, and it is thought that the list was conceived as a sort of tourist itinerary.

Alone of the Seven Wonders, only the Pyramids have survived intact. Over the centuries since Philon and Antipatros described them (probably in about 150 BC and 100 BC respectively), the other six have been despoiled or demolished.

Hands off the Colossus

The Colossus was a gigantic statue, probably of Helios, the Greek sun god, erected by the citizens of the island of Rhodes in the Aegean Sea to celebrate the lifting of a year-long siege by the Macedonians in about 304 BC.

Exact details of its history and construction are vague – for example, we don't know exactly where it stood – but the Colossus was probably completed in 280 BC and took no less than twenty-four years to build. It was at least 100 feet tall. The historian Pliny the Elder provides the best clue to its scale and impact: 'Few men can embrace its thumb, its fingers are larger than most statues.'

Sadly, no accurate description of the statue's appearance has come down to us, but the god seems to have been portrayed as a standing figure set on a base of white marble. Much of his body was apparently covered with huge sheets of bronze over a framework of stones and iron rods.

Despite the figure's undoubted size, it is unlikely that there is any truth in the legend that the Colossus stood astride the entrance to one of the two harbours of Rhodes: in all probability the engineering problems would have defeated the builders, and the giant's legs would have had to have been grotesquely out of proportion to the rest of his body.

What does seem certain is that the Colossus stood in all its glory for only a very short time – just over half a century. A huge earthquake in about 224 BC brought it down, and its ruins lay neglected as the people of Rhodes concentrated upon rebuilding their homes and temples. But even prostrate on the ground the Colossus was still an object of wonder, and almost 900 years passed before its bronze 'skin' was sold for scrap by Arab invaders in the seventh century AD and was taken away on the backs of a caravan of camels – 90 or 900, depending upon how you interpret contemporary accounts.

Hunting for the Hunter's temple

The scattered stones which are all that now remain of the Temple of Diana at Ephesus in western Turkey belie the magnificence that made the building a magnet for travellers and pilgrims.

Once again, the exact details of what the temple looked like have not come down to us, but it was apparently constructed of white marble and cypress and cedar wood, and decorated with statues, paintings and friezes, its lofty roof supported by rows of imposing columns, some elaborately carved with religious scenes. An earlier temple on the site had been destroyed by an arsonist called Herostratos in 356 BC, on the very night, it was said, that Alexander the Great was born. Remarkably, it was Alexander who commissioned the replacement – the one that qualified as one of the Seven Wonders – in about 330 BC. The temple was finally destroyed in the Christian era. The *Acts of the Apostles* in the Bible records how St Paul's missionary work initially met with resistance from the followers of Diana, but later the marble that had once dazzled visitors to the temple was borne away and used to build a church. The sculpture and

July 1987. A weird rock is recovered from the sea off Rhodes. Claims that it was a hand of the Colossus were discounted by Greek Culture Minister Melina Mercouri, who said, 'I must say the truth even if it is bitter. It is not the Colossus. It is not even ancient. All the archaeologists of my ministry agree it has nothing to do with the statue.'

Martin van Heemskerk's impression of the Mausoleum at Halicarnassus: one of many attempts to reconstruct a Wonder of which only a few fragments now remain.

paintings that had adorned it were destroyed and the site was gradually reclaimed by the encroaching marshes.

Almost as remarkable as the temple itself is the story of the site's rediscovery. In 1863, the British Museum in London sent to Ephesus a man who rejoiced in the name of John Turtle Wood. Wood's researches amongst descriptions by the writers of ancient times proved to be the key to the mystery, for he discovered a tomb which, according to the old texts, had been sited near the road to the temple. Next, he came upon the road itself. It was lined with sarcophagi. Elated, Wood followed it – only to find that a farmer had planted a field of barley on the very spot where the temple seemed to lie! Time and his British Museum funds were running out, but Wood was determined not to give up, and an excavation on a patch of land not owned by the farmer revealed a wall and two inscriptions which confirmed that one of the Seven Wonders of the World had once stood where the barley was now ripening. Wood promptly bought the field from the farmer for a paltry £160, and the excavation of the complete temple then began.

The mystery of the Mausoleum

The Mausoleum was the last resting place of Mausolos, ruler of Caria, who died in about 350 BC. It was erected by his widow, Artemisia, at Halicarnassus (now the popular holiday destination of Bodrum in Turkey) and was undoubtedly bigger and better than most of the elaborate tombs named after it throughout the succeeding centuries.

Like the Colossus of Rhodes, the Mausoleum seems to have been destroyed by an earthquake and its stones were later re-used in the fifteenth and sixteenth centuries by the Knights of St John to build their castle at Bodrum. So today, all that remains of the Fifth Wonder of the Ancient World is an excavation site and a collection of friezes which the Knights had incorporated into their castle walls. These were later taken down and presented to the British Museum in London in 1846.

What did the Mausoleum look like? Once again no one knows for sure, but plenty of people have made a guess. One, the eighteenth-century architect Nicholas Hawksmoor, incorporated his ideas into his design for the steeple of a London church, St George's, Bloomsbury. Excavations by a team of Danish archaeologists have amplified descriptions left by ancient writers, notably Pliny, and greatly increased modern understanding of the building. A rough consensus seems to be this: on top of a tall rectangular base ran a colonnade, probably with nine pillars at each end and eleven along the sides. Projecting blocks of stone supported a cornice and an elaborate gutter covered in floral decorations and spouts like lion-heads. Above this loomed a stepped pyramid, culminating in a gigantic sculpture of a chariot drawn by four magnificent horses (part of one of them has survived and is in the British Museum).

Light on the lighthouse

Designed by Sostratus of Cnidus in about 270 BC, the Pharos lighthouse was probably about 400 feet high (the tallest in the modern world, at Yamashita Park, Yokohama, Japan, is only 348 ft). It stood on an island just outside the harbour at Alexandria, Egypt. At night the flames of the lighthouse beacon, reflected by huge mirrors, could be seen by approaching sailors from more than thirty miles away. By day, navigators took bearings from the fire's column of smoke.

After being irreparably damaged by an earthquake in 1375, this extraordinary building was 'cannibalised' into a castle and had disappeared completely by 1500.

The wonder of Olympia

The plinth on which the statue of Zeus stood was discovered by German archaeologists during excavations of the Temple of Zeus at Olympia, Greece, in the late nineteenth century. It is all that remains of one of the most impressive statues of the ancient world. Fashioned from ivory and gold, it was a gigantic representation of the most revered of all the Greek gods.

The Hanging Gardens

The Hanging Gardens of Babylon were the most exotic of the Seven Wonders. The city stood by the River Euphrates to the south of the modern city of Baghdad, capital of Iraq.

No one knows exactly what the gardens looked like, although it is probable that they were terraced, as opposed to somehow hanging in the air. Nor has their location been definitely found, although a German archaeologist, Robert Koldewey, claimed to have uncovered the remains of a likely building at the turn of the century. This contained a curious well, unlike any other in the ruins of Babylon, and its shape suggested to Koldewey that water may have been pumped to the upper levels of the vaulted building in which it had been sunk.

13

Unconventional conventions

You can depend on the Americans to think up the strangest gatherings. In 1984, the editor of a magazine no Jew's-harp player can be without (it's snappily entitled the *Vierundzwanzigsteljahrschrift der Internationalen Maultrommelvirtuosengenossenschaft*) organised the first **International Jew's-Harp Congress** in Utah. On the agenda for discussion was the public 'image' of the instrument's devotees, who tend to be treated like 'flat-earth people,' according to one tetchy twanger.

There's even a convention for the **Bald-Headed Men of America**, an organisation that boasts 10,000 shiny-pated members. They take consolation from the knowledge that Julius Caesar and Shakespeare feature amongst the Great Baldies of History. One major decision taken at the 1984 convention was to admit six women to membership, and in 1990 the convention acclaimed a member from West Virginia for having the year's Most Kissable Bald Head.

At Britt, Iowa, they've been holding an annual **Hobo Convention** since the beginning of the century. Huge crowds turn out to watch the crowning of the king and queen of the hobos, and the unpredictable behaviour of the ladies and gentlemen of the road simply adds to the fun.

At Wayne, Nebraska, they know the answer to an old, old riddle:

Q: Why did the chicken cross the road?
A: To get the the **Wayne Hen-ual Chicken Show**.

Attractions include chicken chariot races and the 'national cluck-off' – whatever that may be.

But our favourite conventions are the **Cowboy Poetry Gatherings** where gnarled cowpokes assemble to recite verses composed as they ride the range. A typical gathering was held in 1986 in Elko, Nevada, described by one authority as 'the last real cow-town in the West'. Today's cowboy thinks ecological thoughts if these verses, *Reincarnation* by Montana rancher Wallace McRae, are anything to go by:

'What does reincarnation mean?'
A cowpoke ast his friend.
His pal replied, 'It happens when
Yer life has reached its end.
They comb yer hair, and warsh yer neck,
And clean yer fingernails,
And lay you in a padded box
Away from life's travails.

'The box and you goes in a hole,
That's been dug into the ground.
Reincarnation starts in when
Yore planted 'neath a mound.
Them clods melt down, just like yer box,
And you who is inside.
And then yore just beginnin' on
Yer transformation ride.

'In a while the grass'll grow
Upon yer rendered mound.
Till some day on your moldered grave
A lonely flower is found.
And say a hoss should wander by
And graze upon this flower
That once wuz you, but now's become
Yer vegetative bower.

'The posy that the hoss done ate
Up, with his other feed,
Makes bone, and fat, and muscle
Essential to the steed.
But some is left that he can't use
And so it passes through,
And finally lays upon the ground.
This thing, that once wuz you.

'Then say, by chance, I wanders by
And sees this upon the ground,
And I ponders and I wonders at,
This object that I found.

I thinks of reincarnation,
Of life, and death, and such,
And come away concludin': "Slim,
YOU AIN'T CHANGED, ALL THAT MUCH."'

14

Human Sacrifice

The terrible urge of human beings to sacrifice their fellow men to appease whatever dark gods possess their imagination still persists in modern times.

In India today sacrifices still surface. In 1987 the fearsome practitioners of Thuggee reappeared. The British rulers of India in the last century waged a constant struggle against the Thugs, who believed that the murder of travellers was a regular requirement to satisfy the appetites of their gods. The Thugs themselves were captured and executed, and the British believed they had defeated the cult. But in the 1980s there were scattered reports that the practice had survived. And then, in 1987, a terrified witness testified that the cult's devotees were once again seeking their victims among travellers in the dark along the dusty Indian roads. A young Indian worker was suddenly assaulted as he walked home in Uttar Pradesh. He was taken to a remote spot where the ritual began. Then, bound hand and foot, he was finally beheaded.

In the state of Orissa, not long before, a boy of eight had been taken to a temple dedicated to the goddess Durga by a group of men who wished to be liberated from ghosts that they believed were haunting them. There, in front of the deity, he was stabbed to death.

Ritual sacrifice in any era can be an elaborate business. In Britain the Sutton Hoo excavation in Suffolk is starting to uncover the dark customs of the Anglo-Saxon pagans.

Near the spot where the great Anglo-Saxon king's ship was found buried in 1939, complete with his beautiful gold helmet and finely worked armour and the goods and chattels for the next life, the archaeologists found two victims with their wrists tied behind their backs. Two more were buried kneeling – one with the top of his skull sliced off by a blow. Another has his hands tied above his head. A further one has his neck broken.

Strangest of all seems to be the ploughman and his plough, sacrificed perhaps to seek good seed-time and harvest. The large grave seems to have been dug specially to receive him. The plough is in place. The man has his leg splayed as if to guide it through the furrow. Thus, apparently, he met his death.

When the tomb of a Chinese emperor, Wen Di, who lived in the second century BC, was discovered in 1983, it was found to contain the bodies of six servants who had been sacrificed to look after the emperor after his death. Nearby, were the remains of four of the great man's concubines, killed to keep him company in the afterlife.

In prehistoric Britain, the victims of human sacrifice were often small children. During excavations at Woodhenge, part of the great Stonehenge 'complex' in Wiltshire, archaeologists uncovered the skeleton of a four-year-old girl. As a result, presumably, of some grisly ritual, her head had been split open and pointed towards the midsummer sunrise.

Even more horrifying was the sight that met the eyes of archaeologists in South Uist, an island in the Outer Hebrides. In four pits they found the remains of a twelve-year-old boy. Laboratory work showed that he had died, in about 200 BC, as the result of two sharp blows from some kind of knife. The manner of the boy's death and burial suggested to experts that he may have been killed in a 'prediction ritual', for it is known that the Celts believed they could tell the future by watching a person's death agonies.

The discovery of the mummified body of yet another child – this time in South America in 1954 – brought into being a new form of researcher: the mountaineer-archaeologist. The boy, who died some 500 years ago, was found at the top of Cerro Plomo, more than 17,000 feet up in the Chilean Andes. He had been decked out in Inca ceremonial regalia before being walled up to die in a freezing tomb, presumably to appease a mountain god.

Further investigations revealed that children, and even young men, were sacrificed on other mountain peaks in South America. Now their mummified remains are being discovered and studied by a small group of archaeologists with the skills to scale the heights where the brutal ceremonies were enacted in the thin and icy air.

Excavations on the Saxon Ship at Sutton Hoo in 1939. Recent work at the site has uncovered graves which seem to have been specially prepared to take sacrifice victims in ritual positions.

15

Turf talking

For all the care and cossetting of modern training and scientific skills, horses, unlike humans, do not seem to run any faster. The fastest Derby was run more than fifty years ago, won by the grey Mahmoud in 1936 in a time of 2 minutes 33.8 seconds.

But horses do go on racing long after they might have been expected to have departed for other pastures. Creggmore Boy won his first race when he was seventeen and was still running at the age of twenty-two in 1962. He had come second in a race the year before.

Wild Aster won three hurdle races at the age of eighteen within a week in March 1919.

Sonny Somers won two steeplechases in 1980 at the age of eighteen.

The most remarkable winner in racing history was a mare called Kincsem who was bred in Hungary in 1874 and wandered about Europe by train competing wherever there was a suitable race. She had won thirty-six races, including a number of European classics, by the time she arrived in England in 1878. She duly collected the Goodwood Cup, and then, on the way home, the Grand Prix at Deauville and the Grosser Preis at Baden. By the time she was retired the following year, she had won fifty-four races and had never been beaten.

In 1929 the Irish Grand National was won by a jockey wearing an artificial leg. Mr Frank Wise, who rode Alike, a mare which he also owned and trained, had also lost the tops of three fingers on his right hand during the First World War.

16

Curses!

A bizarre collection of charms and amulets in Scotland's National Museum of Antiquities in Edinburgh includes a calf's heart pierced with pins, a pebble used by a fishwife to ward off nightmares and a row of tiny 'fairy coffins' unearthed in the city in 1836. All were designed to fend off evil forces or put a curse upon the head of an enemy. Such practices are common not only in Scotland but throughout the world. Here are a few objects that are said to bring danger to those who handle them and some places where it may be dangerous to linger.

The diamond of disaster

All kinds of misfortunes are said to have overtaken owners of the magnificent Hope Diamond, now in the Smithsonian Institution in Washington, D.C.

According to legend, victims of the Hope Diamond curse include the French gem merchant who brought it to Europe from India – he is said to have lost his fortune and to have been devoured by wild dogs. A Dutch jeweller who recut the diamond apparently died of grief after his son stole the stone, and another of its owners is alleged to have perished of starvation a day after financial ruin forced him to sell it for a pittance. Other stories of the 'curse's' effect abound: a French dealer apparently went mad after buying the diamond, and committed suicide; an actress who borrowed it to wear on stage was shot the next day by her lover; and a Greek jeweller who sold it to a Sultan was killed with his wife and child when his car toppled over a precipice.

Mrs Evalyn McLean bedecked with the Hope Diamond. On less formal occasions it was often worn by her dog.

These 'fairy coffins', thought to have been designed to ward off evil, were found buried on a hill in Edinburgh in 1836.

Sadly, these tales all seem to be nonsense. Many may have been invented by a clever salesman in about 1910 to attract a particular buyer, for it was known that Mrs Evalyn McLean often said that things that brought other people bad luck proved lucky for her. Not in this case, however, for, after she had bought the Hope Diamond, her eldest son and her only daughter died tragically and her husband was declared insane. Yet Mrs McLean never blamed the Hope Diamond for her misfortunes. Instead, it seems to have given her pleasure which she gladly shared. For example, on hospital visits during the Second World War, she let wounded servicemen play catch with it, and the great Hope Diamond even adorned the collar of Mike, her dog.

Tomb and doom

Curses placed on tombs serve a useful purpose: they keep the grave robbers away. But do they really work? Consider two tales.

In Cracow, Poland, scientists and historians dropped like flies after the city's cardinal, Karol Wojtyla, later Pope John Paul II, allowed the tomb of King Casimir IV to be opened after 500 years. At least ten people died after visiting the King's last resting-place in Wawel Castle.

In New York in 1979 an art restorer fell ill while working on a tapestry excavated from a Peruvian grave.

A Polish historian, Zbigniew Swiech, investigated Casimir's Curse and in 1983 published a book, *Curses, Germs and Scientists*, in which he suggested that the curse's 'victims' had been killed by a 500-year-old microbe which had been sealed up in the tomb along with King Casimir.

The 'curse' of the Peruvian tapestry was also explained – and its 'victim' saved – thanks to some doughty detective-work. The tapestry restorer was already ill with cramps, dizziness and a distressing burning sensation in her abdomen before Dr Alf Fischbein of Mount Sinai Medical Centre, New York, hit upon the causes of her malady. Not only had she been working in a poorly ventilated room, she had also been coating the tapestry with some red powder found in the tomb. Analysis revealed that this contained red lead, and the restorer's habit of licking the thread with which she had been mending the tapestry had caused her to swallow lead in poisonous amounts. All curse theories were forgotten and the woman was successfully treated for lead poisoning.

The Fyvie curse

The curse of Fyvie Castle, Aberdeenshire, is the most sinister of the many maledictions against some of Scotland's noblest houses pronounced by a shadowy figure known as 'True Tammas' or 'Thomas the Rhymer'. A visit from Thomas was something no one forgot in a hurry – or usually for many generations, for he tended to curse a place and the family that owned it before he had hardly crossed the threshold.

The sinister seer is said to have appeared at Fyvie in dramatic circumstances sometime during the thirteenth century. According to one account:

> he suddenly appeared before the fair building, accompanied by a violent storm of wind and rain, which stripped the surrounding trees of their leaves, and shut the Castle gates with a loud crash. But while the tempest was raging on all sides, it was observed that, close by the spot where Tammas stood, there was not wind enough to shake a pile of grass or a hair of his beard.

In mid-tempest, he declaimed this doom-laden ditty:

> Fyvie, Fyvie thou's never thrive,
> As lang's there's in the stanis three;
> There's ane intill the oldest tower,
> There's ane intill the ladye's bower,
> There's ane intill the water-yett,
> And thir three stanes ye's never get.

What this meant, in English, was that the inhabitants of Fyvie would be cursed until they had managed to bring together three stones: one somewhere in the castle's oldest tower, one in the lady's 'bower,' and the third somewhere by the water-gate in the river.

To this day, only one has been found, and ill-luck has befallen the denizens of Fyvie. Since 1885 no eldest son has lived to succeed to the castle and its lands.

The cursed car

All kinds of dreadful fates are said to have overtaken people who went near, or even bought parts of, the Porsche Spyder car in which film star James Dean was killed in September 1955. Among the reported incidents:

The remains of the Porsche in which James Dean met his death in 1955. Dreadful fates are said to have overtaken people who have had anything to do with the car since.

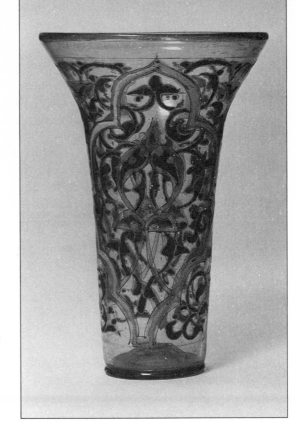

The Luck of Edenhall (right) inspired a fashion for such talismans among the English landed gentry. Thus, one family treasured a glass bowl known as the Luck of Muncaster, and another a cup called the Luck of Workington.

a mechanic and one of Dean's fans were apparently injured when the car fell on them in separate accidents; a racing driver who had bought the engine for his own vehicle died in a crash; and a garage in which the Spyder was parked overnight went up in flames.

Did actor Sir Alec Guinness sense there was something doomed about Dean's car? In his memoirs *Blessings In Disguise* Guinness tells of a chance meeting with Dean in a Los Angeles restaurant in September 1955. Guinness had gone there with a scriptwriter, Thelma Moss, after a long and tiring flight from Europe. When the young man proudly showed him the sportscar, which had just been delivered and was in the restaurant parking lot, a curious sensation came over the distinguished British actor.

I heard myself saying in a voice I could hardly recognise as my own, 'Please never get in it.' I looked at my watch. 'It is now ten o'clock, Friday the 23rd of September, 1955. If you get in that car you will be found dead in it by this time next week.'

The following Friday, Dean died at the wheel of his new car.

One for luck

With so many curses about, it is not surprising that talismans and other objects reputed to have the power to scare off evil spirits have traditionally proved popular.

Perhaps the most famous is the Luck of Edenhall, a beautiful glass beaker which used to be owned by the Musgrave family of Edenhall, an imposing mansion in Cumbria. According to legend, it was found by the Musgraves' butler, who had surprised some thirsty fairies at a well. As the little people fled, one is said to have uttered the dire warning:

> If this cup should break or fall,
> Farewell the Luck of Edenhall.

The Luck is gilded and wonderfully decorated with red, green, white and blue enamelling and was probably made in Syria in the thirteenth century. In 1926 the Musgraves lent their precious glass to London's Victoria and Albert Museum. Eight years later the house was demolished. Had the loan activated the fairies' curse? The museum, which acquired the Luck in 1958, has been careful never to allow it to 'break or fall'.

The bleeding harbinger

Finally, the curious case of a creature which in death seems able to predict disaster for the living.

The Grant-Sturgis family of Devon owns a mummified hawk which is an apparently unfailing predictor of war. When hostilities are planned against England by some foreign power, blood is said to seep from the small brown bird which is $10\frac{1}{2}$ inches long and weighs $7\frac{1}{2}$ ounces.

The hawk was brought to Devon from Egypt in 1887 by an explorer named W. J. A. Grant. It first bled just before the Boer War and continued to do so until peace was declared. In 1914, ten days before the First World War broke out, the bird began to bleed again. Only when the Armistice was signed four years later did it dry up. Robert Baden-Powell, the British general and founder of the Boy Scouts, is said to have witnessed the phenomenon and to have been amazed by what he saw.

Between the wars, another soldier visiting Mr Grant was reassured when, despite his prophecies of the imminence of another conflict, the hawk remained dry. 1939 would have provided another major test of the bird's forecasting abilities, but by then Mr Grant's home had been requisitioned by the government and its contents – including the hawk – put into storage.

17

Dead – and call me
mummy . . .

It's fun to gaze upon the face of one of history's most notorious figures. No lover of the curious visiting Moscow would dream of missing the chance of viewing the body of Vladimir Ilich Lenin, the Soviet Union's first leader: along with the State Circus and St Basil's Cathedral, it's one of the great tourist attractions of the city. Lenin's squat mausoleum below the Kremlin walls is open only between 10 am and 1 pm on weekdays, and long queues (jumpable by tourists if their Intourist guide is feeling friendly) stretch down Red Square past the History Museum and out into the Moscow streets. After Lenin's death in 1924 great pains were taken to preserve his body and he was carefully embalmed. It is said that the recently discovered mummy of Tutankhamun suggested the idea to the Commission for the Immortalization of the Memory of V. I. Ulyanov (Lenin). In Peking, the body of that other great giant of the communist world, Chairman Mao, has also not been allowed to crumble to dust, thanks to the wonder of the refrigerator. He, too, in death, is a tourist attraction.

But don't worry if you can't get to Moscow or Peking. The world is full of preserved bodies (although one expert in 1985 warned that the world was down to its last thousand actual mummies, because so many had been ground down to make medicines and even locomotive fuel), and you may well find one in a casket, glass case or graveyard near you. That said, we start our pilgrimage to the preserved in the remote mountains of Papua New Guinea . . .

The tribe that smokes its dead

Travellers who have managed to penetrate the jungle-clad mountains of Morobe Province, Papua New Guinea, report a bizarre and grisly sight: the smoked bodies of dead villagers ranged along a granite ledge beneath a cliff.

Explorer Christina Dodwell took time off from an expedition to the Waghi River to pay her respects to the long-dead citizens of Kokea village. Her guide was Giami, the local headman.

> We rounded a rocky outcrop and suddenly I was on a crumbly ledge below an overhanging cliff, [she wrote.] Just in front of me was a line of about ten smoked corpses, sitting with their knees drawn up to their chests, held above ground by a row of open baskets propped up on poles. Giami said that most of the bodies had been there for centuries, although some were more recent and he pointed to one shrunken body which he said was brought there fourteen years ago. Its dry, red-ochred skin was shrivelled, and looked like parchment: its skull was propped up by an arrow and its empty eye-sockets stared out at the world.
>
> According to Giami, the man had been a *bigman* called Moaymungo, and after his death his family had smoke-cured his corpse for several months in a smoke-house, like a ham, before carrying it up to its place there. People believe that the ancestor-spirits watch over their descendants and protect them.

The Atacama mummies

There are few better places on earth for preserving bodies than the Atacama desert of South America. It has hardly ever rained there in all recorded history, and the Atacama's hot soil helps to keep flesh dry and unrotted on the bone.

In 1983 an extraordinary graveyard was found by building workers at the village of Arica on the edge of the Atacama. It contained the mummified bodies of Chinciro Indians who lived and died about 10,000 years ago. Most astonishing of all is evidence that the Chinciros perfected sophisticated mummification techniques 7,000 years before the Egyptians.

Here's the Chinciro recipe for a long-lasting mummy. Take one dead person and peel the skin from the body. Then leave it out in the sun to dry before curing it over a fire. Meanwhile, clean the skeleton and stuff it

Chinciro mummies, once cured, were propped up with a stick and set out on a hillside to keep watch over the Pacific Ocean.

with mud or shells. Next, sew the skin back on. If it fails to fit properly, patch it with any skin – from animals or birds – you can lay hands on. Finally, place a mask over the skull, paint the body to make it look life-like, prop it up with a stick, and leave for several thousand years,,,

Caruso's corpse

Not everybody likes the idea of displaying preserved bodies. That's why the great Italian opera singer Enrico Caruso can no longer be viewed in a transparent coffin. When he died in 1921, 100,000 of his fans lined the route of the funeral cortège to the Del Planto cemetery in Naples, and many others later flocked to inspect their hero.

Every year after that, for five years, his clothes were changed to ensure that he looked spick and span for his adoring visitors. But his widow thought the arrangement unseemly, and in 1927 the body was removed and placed in a tomb, out of sight of the curious.

Arctic mummies

The ice and frozen earth of the Arctic offer ideal conditions for preserving bodies. Eight preserved bodies were discovered at Qilakitsoq, Greenland, in 1972. Two ptarmigan hunters, Hans and Jokum Grønvold, found them after moving some stones which they noticed had been laid out in an unusual way. The bodies were those of Inuits who had presumably lived in a settlement nearby. Carbon-dating by scientists at Denmark's National Museum in Copenhagen established that the six women and two children had died in about 1475; yet after five hundred years their limbs and clothes were intact and the remains of a meal had been preserved in the guts of one of them. Most touching of all were the mummified remains of a baby, aged about six months, still dressed in his little fur anorak, sealskin leggings, and grass-lined boots. This was the best preserved of the bodies; in fact the ptarmigan hunters had originally thought it was a doll. One of the researchers, Jens P. Hat Hansen, explained why it had survived so well:

> ... in the early stages of decomposition body heat is a key factor. The higher the body's inside temperature, the greater the bacterial action and consequent breakdown of tissue. Thus, people who die with high

fever tend to decompose rapidly, as do overweight people, whose insulating layer of fat retains body heat for a longer period. Children tend to decompose the most slowly, for their body volume is small compared with the skin area, providing for rapid dissipation of heat.

Dead Speedy

Speedy Atkins' appearance on the popular American television show 'That's Incredible' ranks high on our list of Great Moments In Television. Speedy died in 1928 after falling into a river while fishing. No one came forward to claim his body. Officials of the Hamock Funeral Home in Paducah, Kentucky, were touched by Speedy's plight, however, and all the skills of their best embalmer were lavished upon him. The morticians did such a fine job that they couldn't bear to bury Speedy's body, and decided to keep him around.

For the television show, Speedy was flown across the United States to California with his entourage. First Class, of course.

Bentham's bones

Jeremy Bentham, an eighteenth-century writer and philosopher, wanted to prove a point when he left his body to University College, London, where it is still on display, decked out in his favourite clothes, complete with straw hat and walking stick, more than 150 years after his death.

Behind Bentham's instructions lay years of meditation on the usefulness of the dead to the living. A year or two before he died, Bentham wrote a treatise called *Auto-Icon, or the Uses of the Dead to the Living*. In it he suggested that dead bodies should be embalmed and varnished so that everyone could be their own statue or auto-icon. They could then, for example, be used to decorate people's gardens and remind their descendants of their forebears. Although Bentham had the theory all worked out, in practice the preservation of his own body did not work out as well as he had hoped; his head deteriorated so much that it had to be replaced with a wax mask.

Thus adorned, Bentham's body was brought into meetings of the governing body of University College – a bizarre practice that lasted more than ninety years. His presence was always noted and respected, but he was never, in death, allowed a vote.

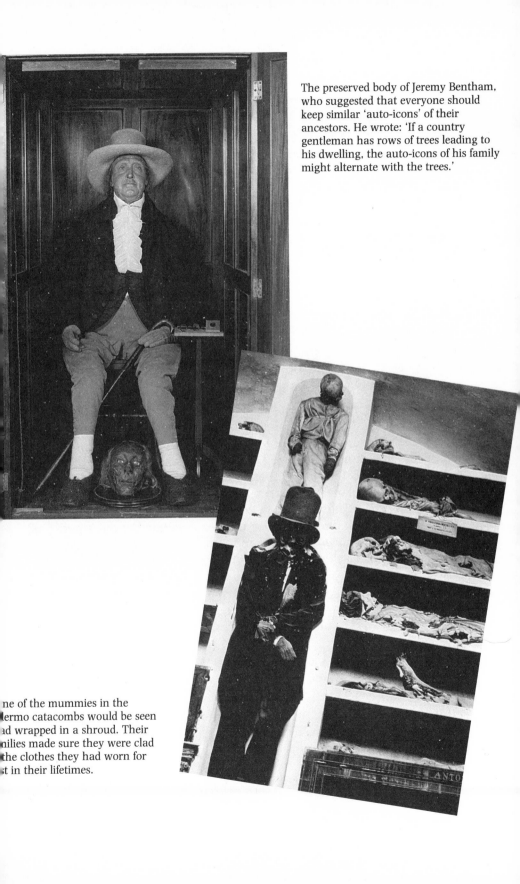

The preserved body of Jeremy Bentham, who suggested that everyone should keep similar 'auto-icons' of their ancestors. He wrote: 'If a country gentleman has rows of trees leading to his dwelling, the auto-icons of his family might alternate with the trees.'

ne of the mummies in the [P]ermo catacombs would be seen [cl]ad wrapped in a shroud. Their [fa]milies made sure they were clad [in] the clothes they had worn for [be]st in their lifetimes.

The mummies in the catacombs

For a small donation to convent funds, visitors to Sicily can view dozens of mummified islanders at the Convent of the Cappuccini off the Via Cipressi in Palermo. The microclimate of the catacombs in which they were laid to rest preserves bodies naturally. Though entire families grin down from the walls, there's nothing creepy about the array of corpses, although the way in which some of them seem to be straining against the ropes that hold them up can be unnerving. At the end of your stroll through the corpse-covered corridors, you can buy lurid postcards of the dear departed from a friar; connoisseurs of the curious will of course leave with a sheaf-ful.

The Italian bride

Near the grave of that notorious gangster Al Capone in Mount Carmel Cemetery, Chicago, stands a monument to Julia Buccola Petta, known as the 'Italian bride'. On the plinth beneath the marble figure of a buxom girl in her wedding dress are two photographs in oval frames. One portrays Julia on the day of her marriage. The other is far stranger: it shows her lying dead in her coffin, arrayed once more in her wedding finery. The bloom of life still seems to be upon her cheeks, yet the photograph was taken six years *after* Julia's death in childbirth in 1921.

Her body was exhumed after her mother had experienced a series of weird dreams in which Julia appeared and begged her to persuade the authorities to allow the grave to be reopened. Permission was finally granted in 1927, six years after Julia's burial. And when the coffin was opened her corpse was found to be in perfect condition: unblemished sweet-smelling, seraphic – it was as though she had just died.

Saints alive! Dead saints!

Nothing adds more to the reputation of a saint than the discovery that his or her dead body has remained unaffected by the normal processes of decay. Over the centuries, church historians have described many examples of incorruption.

One remarkable preserved body, still on display today in a glass urn in the church of San Geremia and Santa Lucia in Venice, belongs to St Lucy of Syracuse. Lucy met her martyrdom in AD304 because she refused to marry a heathen youth and instead preferred to distribute her dowry to the poor. So vicious were the methods by which the authorities tried to kill her that it is surprising her body remained in one piece to be buried, let alone mummified: she was sentenced to be torn to pieces by oxen, but the gentle beasts refused to move when ordered; later, when pitch and faggots were piled around her, the bonfire failed to catch. She was finally despatched with a knife to her throat. Apart from her face, now decently covered with a silver mask to hide its deterioration, and loss of a scrap of her flesh (now revered in Vienna, Austria), Lucy is in good shape after more than 1600 years.

The body of St Francis Xavier, which is kept in the Basilica of Bom Jesus in Goa, India, is said to be faring less well, although more than a dozen public expositions since his death in 1552 have testified to its remarkable state of preservation.

St Francis was a Spanish missionary who died in China. Since the journey back to Goa was a long one, his followers assumed that the best way to transport his body for burial would be to strip it of its flesh by burying it in quicklime. But when the time for exhumation came, the saint's corpse was as fresh as the day it had first been immersed in the quicklime. Despite another attempt at the quicklime treatment, the amputation of his right arm and its distribution in several pieces to churches in Rome and the East, and an extraordinary assault by an aristocratic Portuguese lady who bit off the little toe of his right foot, St Francis Xavier's body seemed unaffected by the passage of four centuries.

At the 1974 exposition, however, journalist Phillip Knightley, aware of rumours that decay had at last set in, took a close look.

> The body, [he wrote,] is not a pleasant sight. The head, the feet, and one hand are the only parts exposed. The rest is clothed in vestments, partly, it is said, to conceal wires which help hold it together. The skin of the head is shrivelled and pitted, hard in texture, and dark in colour. A powdery, sand-like substance covers most of it, but here and there bone is exposed. Wisps of hair are still visible.

There were rumours during Knightley's visit that the expositions of the body could no longer continue, but between November 1984 and January 1985 it was once again on display, allowing an estimated 100,000 pilgrims to contemplate a saint who in death seems to have outwitted time.

One of the most famous of the 'Incorruptibles' is St Bernadette of Lourdes, the girl whose visions of the Virgin Mary made Lourdes a place of pilgrimage for the sick. In 1909, thirty years after her death, Bernadette's body was shown to astonished followers at the Convent of St Gildard, Nevers, France. Wrote one:

> Not the least trace of corruption nor any bad odour could be perceived in the corpse of our beloved sister. Even the habit in which she was buried was intact. The face was somewhat brown, the eyes slightly sunken, and she seemed to be sleeping. The damp funeral garments were exchanged for new ones. The body was placed in a new zinc coffin lined with white silk. Within it was placed a record enclosed in a glass tube and giving an account of the opening of the coffin and the condition of the body. After this the coffin was again deposited in the mortuary chapel in our garden.

That account was quoted by the greatest authority on the phenomenon of incorruption, Father Herbert Thurston. Thurston's attempts to understand the process of natural mummification went far beyond the call of even a Jesuit's duty. When, for example, he was studying adipocere, the soapy substance that human flesh can turn into after burial, he kept some at home wrapped in brown paper.

Thurston never could decide on the answer to the question: is the preservation of a saint's body due to natural or supernatural causes? He quotes the case of Blessed Maria Anna (Ladroni) of Jesus who died in 1624, and whose body upon exhumation some years later was, according to the Bishop of Malaga, 'so completely preserved that neither in the abdomen nor in the face was there any trace of decay, except a spot on the lip, though this was something by which she had been marked in much the same way during life.

A second examination, 107 years after the Blessed Maria's death, found no change in her condition, and the probing scalpels of the 'eleven professors of medicine and surgery, all of them among the first and most famous in the city and court of Madrid' found that 'the interior organs, the viscera and the fleshy tissues were all of them entire, sound, moist and resilient'. Yet Thurston noted that there did seem to be an element of the miraculous and supernatural in the body's survival, for the 'other corpses which had been buried in the same vault had all been subject to the common law of decay'.

Miscellaneous mummies in Britain

Cambridge University's Faculty of Archaeology and Anthropology possesses the mummified remains of one of the Guanche people who inhabited the Canary Islands in ancient times. The mummy, though emasculated and rather raddled, is impressive and has a fine head of hair. It was found by a sailor in the 1770s in a cave. He persuaded the authorities to allow him to bring the corpse back to England, where archaeologists discovered that it had been embalmed rather like an Egyptian mummy: its intestines had been replaced with stuffing.

Even more striking is the body, probably of a medieval monk, which was discovered during excavations at St Bees Priory, Cumbria, in the north of England in 1981. Inside its coffin, the cadaver was wrapped in lead. So well had it weathered the centuries – the graveyard was in use between 1120 and 1300 – that liquid, which looked remarkably like fresh blood, flowed when the body was cut open for examination. After the autopsy, the body was reburied: no one can tell whether it will remain incorrupt for another few hundred years.

Down among the bogmen

Peat-bogs offer a good, if not perfect, environment for the preservation of bodies: lack of oxygen prevents flesh from rotting, and the acidity of the water is uncongenial to the micro-organisms that cause decay. Some corpses have looked so fresh after being dug out of their boggy grave, that they have at first been taken for modern murder victims. When the body of an Iron Age man was discovered in Lindow Moss, a bog in the north of England, in 1986, it was confined to a nearby hospital mortuary until the archaeological dating experts had satisfied the authorities that the man, nicknamed 'Pete Marsh' by the press, had died in ancient times. No one had forgotten how the discovery of a woman's head in the same bog a year earlier had panicked a man into confessing to the previously unsuspected murder of his wife! By the time the archaeologists had calculated that the woman to whom the head belonged had died in about AD 210 the machinery of the law was already in motion.

Tollund Man is perhaps the world's most famous bog burial. His body, on display at the Silkeborg Museum, Denmark, was discovered in Tollund Fen, Denmark, in 1950. Tollund man is an eerie sight, for he is naked, save for a leather cap on his head and a belt round his waist. His face is

St Francis Xavier at rest in Goa. Until the twentieth century, his body seemed to have been miraculou⸱ preserved. Now decay seems to have set in.

Tollund Man. His body was so well preserved by the wet peat in which he was buried that the grisly evidence of how he met his death is still clear to see.

peaceful, as though he welcomed death when it came more than 2,000 years ago. Yet firmly knotted round his neck is a leather rope: he had been strangled, perhaps as part of a fertility rite, designed to ensure good crops for the coming year.

Pete Marsh and Tollund Man are two of at least 700 bodies, in varying states of preservation, which have been found in European bogs – more than a hundred of them in Britain alone. Among the best-preserved is Grauballe Man in the Forhistorisk Museum, Moesgord, Denmark. Grauballe Man was found, also by peat cutters, in 1952. The deep slash across his throat suggests that he, too, was murdered. From another Danish bog, Borre Fen, comes an even more touching corpse – of a woman covered with a cloth and and shawl but otherwise naked. Near her were the pitiful remains of a new-born baby.

The case of the stuffed retainer

Finally, a preserved body immortalised in an unforgettable paragraph in an account of a visit to India by a film maker called Stephen Weeks. One day he entered the Maharajah of Mysore's palace in Bangalore, and this is what he found:

> In a glass case in the main entrance of the palace was a stuffed footman. There was an inscription on the case, saying that he had started as an under-gardener, risen to head-gardener, and then been made footman; and he'd given 27 years' loyal service. There's something rather eerie about having a favourite retainer immortalised in a glass case; it is not the kind of thing you'd see in England.

18

Mona Lisa – curiosities to make you smile

The Mona Lisa is the most famous picture in the world. It was painted by Leonardo da Vinci and hangs in the Louvre in Paris. Almost everything else about it is uncertain – Whom does it portray? Why is the lady smiling? Exactly when did Leonardo begin and finish the picture? – except that the Mona Lisa has inspired all kinds of curious theories, events and copies.

A sickly smile?

What is the secret of the Mona Lisa's smile? Was the model who sat for Leonardo da Vinci simply enjoying a joke like all those partygoers in society magazines?

Or was Leonardo rather inexpert at drawing lips, as one theory has it, and her mouth just came out crooked?

Or was it fashionable, as some contemporary sources suggest, for well-brought-up ladies to wear a lop-sided smile?

Or was it a symptom of illness? Several physicians have argued that the smile was induced by a medical condition. For example, when a Dr Nakamura of Tokyo looked into Mona Lisa's eyes, he saw not limpid pools of ageless beauty but a sinister yellowing. This can indicate a build-up of cholesterol, which could mean she was heading for a heart attack. Expanding on this theory, developed after long hours spent examining the picture,

Dr Nakamura said: 'She must have been eating all the wrong foods. She has a nice smile – but soon she would have had nothing to be happy about.'

Californian specialist Dr Kedar Adour came up with a different diagnosis in 1987. He suggested the lady was suffering from a problem with her facial nerves, known as Bell's Palsy. This could have caused a muscle contracture on the left side of her face, leaving her smile a little higher on the left than on the right.

Or was she simply pregnant and feeling rather smug about it? In 1974 Dr Kenneth D. Keele of London claimed in a magazine article that the picture 'probably portrays a pregnant woman whose smile betrays her secret satisfaction and whose full rounded face and figure and beautiful unjewelled hands reveal to a diagnostic eye the endocrine and electrolyte changes of pregnancy'.

* * *

Is there more to Mona than meets the eye?

Did Mona Lisa once wear a necklace? Evidence that she did was put forward by Dr John Asmus of the University of California at San Diego in 1987. The discovery came about while Dr Asmus and his colleagues were making a computer analysis of the painting, designed to establish what it had looked like before varnish and centuries of discolouration dimmed the image. A series of bead-like dots around Mona Lisa's neck were detected during the investigation. This went some way towards answering a question that had long niggled with art historians: why was Mona Lisa apparently portrayed without a necklace, when all the female subjects of Leonardo's earlier portraits sported one? The question now was: if she had originally had a necklace, why was it painted out?

Another investigation, it was claimed later in 1987, revealed that the face of a different woman lay beneath the surface. Lillian Schwartz, an American researcher, studied X-rays of the picture and asserted: 'The X-ray of the Mona Lisa as we know it doesn't match the painting, so I was sure another model existed.' The hidden face, she deduced, belonged to Isabella of Aragon, the beautiful wife of the Duke of Milan. And the reason for the cover-up? Apparently the original commission was cancelled after the death of the Duke, but Leonardo liked the pose so much that he simply painted in the face of his next subject.

This was Miss Schwartz's second revelation about the Mona Lisa within a few months. Earlier, in December 1986, she had announced that, after comparing the smiling lady with a self-portrait by Leonardo, she had come to the amazing conclusion that the face of the Mona Lisa was the mirror-image of the hirsute artist's own. A self-portrait, in fact, of the master in drag.

Is the Mona Lisa in the Louvre the real Mona Lisa?

The Mona Lisa was stolen from the Louvre in 1911 and fakes purporting to be the vanished masterpiece were offered to crooked collectors. However, the thief, Vincenzo Perugia, who had kept the picture in a false-bottomed case, virtually gave himself up to the Italian authorities two years later, and the picture was returned to Paris.

But assuming the painting now hanging in the Louvre is the same one that was there before the robbery (and there are few doubts that it is), is it the picture known as the Mona Lisa in Leonardo's time? 'No,' said London art gallery owner Dr Henry Pulitzer in a book called *Where is the Mona Lisa?* in 1967. Dr Pulitzer claimed that he had bought the *real* Mona Lisa a few years earlier, and argued that Leonardo had painted two similar pictures, one of Monna Lisa Gherardini, the wife of Francesco del Giocondo, and the other of the mistress of one of the Medicis, who was also known as 'La Gioconda'.

According to Dr Pulitzer, the portrait of the mistress ended up in the Louvre after being bought by King Francis I of France in 1517, while the portrait of Monna Lisa del Giocondo became the property of successive private collectors.

Dr Pulitzer's picture is by no means the only 'alternative' Mona Lisa. In 1972 Lord Brownlow offered to lend a version to a London exhibition. There are also several nude Monas around, wearing nothing but a smile, including one in the Chantilly Museum, France. Most 'alternative'of all, perhaps, is the portrait of surrealist artist Salvador Dali as Mona Lisa, complete with curly moustache. But no one is likely to confuse *that* with Leonardo's original!

'alternative' Mona Lisa, wearing nothing but a smile, from the Chantilly Museum, France.

19

Catch a falling star – marvellous meteorites

On the shores of Jackson Lake, Wyoming, USA, on 10 August 1972, a quick-witted photographer snapped a picture of a fireball streaking across the rugged Tetons. It was also spotted as far south as Utah and as far north as Alberta. Although tales of its appearance sparked off the inevitable UFO flap, astronomers were able to identify the fireball's origin with ease. It was a huge meteorite, weighing up to 1,000 tons. Somehow it had just missed colliding with the earth. If it *had* struck, a devastating explosion would have been unleashed – probably as big as that caused by a small nuclear bomb.

Fortunately for our planet, such massive meteorites seldom come so close. Yet earth is under constant bombardment from smaller ones: huge craters all over the world testify to catastrophic impacts in the distant past – some are in remote regions, one is beneath that most frequented hub of modern civilization, O'Hare International Airport, Chicago.

For centuries the remnants of these strange and often destructive celestial visitors have been sought by researchers who hope to glean from them new clues to the origins of the universe, and have been prized by the less scientific as curiosities cast down from the chaos of the heavens.

Mugged by a meteorite

Mrs E. Hulitt Hodges of Sylacauga, Alabama, is the only human being definitely known to have been struck by a meteorite (although other cases, unverified by scientists, have been reported over the years). The meteorite shot through the roof of her house in November 1954, bounced off her radio set and hit her while she was taking an after lunch nap on a sofa. Fortunately Mrs Hulitt Hodges suffered no serious injuries – just a bad bruising. But she did have to be taken to hospital the next day to recover from the bruises and the shock.

The town struck twice by meteorites

As far as anyone knows, Wethersfield, Connecticut, USA, (population 26,000), is the only town ever to have been struck twice by meteorites. To be struck *once* is almost unheard-of: you can count the number of buildings damaged in this way on the fingers of two hands. (One of them was the Prince Llewellyn Hotel at Beddgelert, Wales, in September 1949.) But to sustain *two* hits...

The first hit on 8 April 1971: that meteorite is now in the Smithsonian Institution in Washington, DC. The second came eleven years later on 8 November 1982. Wanda and Robert Donahue were watching *M*A*S*H** on television when the six-pound lump of rock crashed through the roof and two floors of their house and ended up in the floor of the dining room.

As soon as the news got around, scientists from America's leading institutions made a bee-line for Wethersfield. Said one: 'Meteorites are always a dramatic occurrence, but to have two strike the same town is, well, almost incomprehensible.' It was a sentiment echoed by our friend the scientist and writer Arthur C. Clarke. Arthur was in the United States at the time and sent us details of the Wethersfield phenomenon. He told us: 'This is the *most incredible* event I've ever heard of.'

Cooking your goose – by meteorite

A report that a Canada goose had been struck and killed by a meteorite on 18 March 1987 provoked some excited paragraphs in the British press.

The case was reported by a man and a woman who had been ploughing a field at Foulds Farm, Polebrook, near Oundle, Northamptonshire. According to Richard McKim, a local schoolmaster who passed on the story to the *Journal* of the British Astronomical Society, the eyewitnesses said that they had seen 'a thin, bluish, nearly vertical flash travelling downwards and striking the goose amongst a flock of others as they were taking off from the River Nene...'

The unfortunate goose was photographed and duly appeared in the

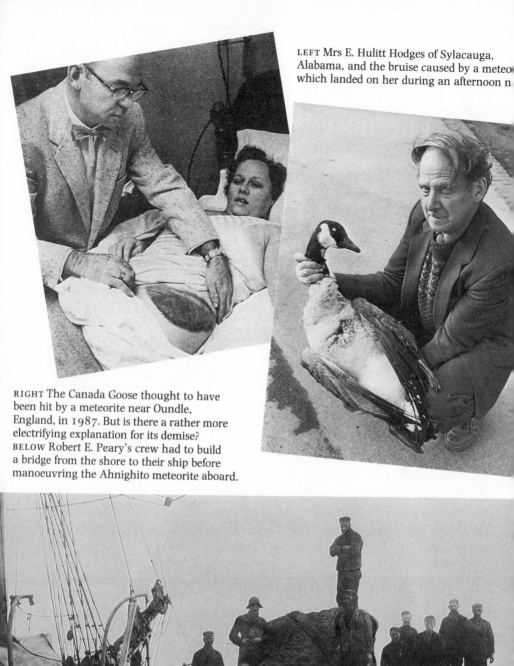

LEFT Mrs E. Hulitt Hodges of Sylacauga, Alabama, and the bruise caused by a meteo[rite] which landed on her during an afternoon n[ap]

RIGHT The Canada Goose thought to have been hit by a meteorite near Oundle, England, in 1987. But is there a rather more electrifying explanation for its demise?
BELOW Robert E. Peary's crew had to build a bridge from the shore to their ship before manoeuvring the Ahnighito meteorite aboard.

local paper which described it as a 'Goose zapped by meteorite in sky'.

But was the caption-writer correct? Richard McKim noted that 'the goose did indeed have two large areas where the feathers had been burnt away, and, within these areas, two holes of a few centimetres in diameter had penetrated the skin'. But a postmortem revealed that 'the wounds were consistent with collision with a relatively thin, mainly horizontal electrically active structure' such as a power line.

A power line did, indeed, run about 150 metres from where the eye-witnesses said the goose had been hit. But how could it have caused the bird's death from such a distance? An electrician named David L. Graham offered a solution to this mystery in a later issue of the same journal. 'I know from direct experience with a sporting gun that a bird shot on the wing can often cover a seemingly amazing distance though technically dead!' he said.

It seems a likely explanation, although no one, as far we know, has calculated the probability of Canada geese being struck by meteorites. Three researchers from the Herzberg Institute of Astrophysics from Ottawa, Canada, have, however, worked out the odds for humans and buildings throughout the entire world. Writing in *Nature* in 1985, they concluded, 'One would ... expect a person to be struck by a meteorite once in nine years and that sixteen buildings per year would receive some damage from meteorites.'

The greatest of them all

The sixty-ton Hoba meteorite, named after the farm on which it was found in 1920, is not in a museum but lies exactly where it fell, probably thousands of years ago, in scrubland near the town of Grootfontein in Namibia, southern Africa. Until 1990, the Hoba meteorite was thought to be the world's largest, but that year Chinese scientists announced the discovery of a real whopper near Shenyang. It was known to local farmers as Huashitai Hill and was 400 ft high.

Peary's prize

In 1907 Robert E. Peary, the great polar explorer, carted another gigantic meteorite off to New York where it is now in the city's American Museum of Natural History.

Known as the Ahnighito or The Tent, it was discovered at Cape York, Greenland, at the beginning of the nineteenth century. From its iron the local people fashioned knifeblades and harpoon tips. When Peary decided to move the meteorite it weighed thirty-four tons, and the problems he faced were formidable. First, the meteorite had to be manhandled the 300 yards to his ship; then Peary had to sail back to New York through treacherous seas without the benefit of a compass: it had been sent crazy by the huge lump of iron.

Crater cartography

The largest authenticated meteorite crater is in northern Arizona, a few miles south of the Interstate 40, between Winslow and Flagstaff. The crater is vast: about 570 feet deep and surrounded by a footpath three miles long. The meteorite that made it may have weighed as much as 300,000 tons. One visiting scientist called it 'the most interesting spot on earth'.

The crater is privately owned, as a result of a mining concession granted by the US government to Daniel Moreau Barringer in 1902. The patent was signed by President Theodore Roosevelt.

Barringer, who spent nearly thirty years at the site, is the only person to have had craters named after him both on the earth (the Barringer Meteorite Crater) and on the moon (the Barringer Lunar Crater, designated by the International Astronomical Union).

The 'Meteorites graveyard'

Antarctica is the place to find meteorites. Until recently, when scientific expeditions began to search seriously for them on the icy continent, only some 2–3,000 fragments had been found in the rest of the world. Now the total from Antarctica is 7,500 and climbing.

The one that got away

In 1924 Captain Ripert, a French officer, reported the discovery of a huge meteorite near Chinguetti in the Adrar desert in the Western Sahara, now part of Mauretania. He broke off a small piece, weighing about four-and-a-half kilos and brought it home to Paris, where it can now be found in the Musée d'Histoire Naturelle, Laboratoire de Minéralogie.

Ripert said that the 'enormous metallic mass measuring about one hundred metres on a side, and about forty metres in height, jutted up in the midst of sand dunes. The visible portion of the surface was vertical, dominating, in the manner of a cliff, the wind-blown sand that was scooped away from the base, so that the summit overhung, and that portion exposed to wind erosion was polished like a mirror.'

The news caused great excitement. But despite the efforts of expeditions to the area, no trace of the Chinguetti meteorite has since been found.

It may, of course, turn up eventually – like the meteorite that was seen to fall near Omsk, USSR, in 1922. Scientists searched everywhere, but without success. Finally, they made a few enquiries amongst the local peasantry, and the missing meteorite was found on a farm, where it was being used as the lid on a barrel of fermenting sauerkraut.

At least they tried

A survey called the Prairie Network, designed to photograph and track meteorites as they fell to earth, recorded only one success in ten years: four fragments recovered near Lost City, Oklahoma, in 1970.

20

Frankenstein's warehouse

Imagine it is midnight. Dr Frankenstein needs a spare part for one of his creations in a hurry. The question is, will he have to wait for one, like the rest of us have to do when we send the television or the car for repair? Of course not. The world is full of limbs and organs which have become detached from the bodies of their original owners. Let's take them from the top...

Hair

Four hairs from the head of the Emperor Napoleon were sold for £280 at a Sotheby's sale in Monte Carlo in the 1980s. They were in a glass tube and had been snipped from the imperial head while Napoleon was in exile on St Helena.

Heads

Our favourite is the head of St Oliver Plunket which is preserved in a splendidly wrought glass case at St Peter's church, Drogheda, Eire. Plunket was martyred in 1681, and his body was divided up by relic-hunters. The saint then went on his travels – in several pieces. As a result, part of an arm is in a convent at Cabra, Spain, but another section of arm was mislaid by absent-minded English monks in Paris. But his clavicle and other bones have now been returned to Drogheda to join his head.

A more recent specimen belonged to the unfortunate George Polk, a well-known American radio correspondent who was killed in Greece. When Polk's body was repatriated by the United States government in 1948, they seem to have left his head behind. It turned up twenty-five years later in a jar back in Greece.

Mr Polk was murdered during the Greek Civil War, apparently while trying to achieve an interview with the leader of the communist insurrection. He was found, bound, gagged and shot in the back, floating in the Gulf of Salonika. And it was at Salonika, in the University's Museum of Criminology, that the head was discovered a quarter of a century later by a Greek reporter. The head was still very recognisable, balding and complete with a bullet-hole in the back of the skull. But how it got into the museum remains a mystery.

Brain

What better brain could there be than Albert Einstein's? Einstein, perhaps the greatest scientist of the twentieth century, died in 1955. His body was cremated and the ashes scattered, but his brain was preserved for postmortem analysis: the great man had specifically requested that it should be made available to researchers in the hope that it would lead to a greater understanding of how the brain works. On hearing of this weird legacy, some doctors wondered whether post-mortem analysis would furnish new insights into that rarest of human qualities, genius.

After Einstein's death, his brain was duly removed at Princeton Medical Center in New Jersey, USA, under the supervision of pathologist Dr Thomas Harvey.

News of the experts' analysis, however, was a long time coming. More than twenty years after Einstein's death, journalist Steven Levy established what had happened to the brain of brains. After the post mortem, Dr Harvey took it, preserved in a jar, to Philadelphia where sections were carefully sliced from it. These were then sent or delivered to specialists around the country.

Eventually, in the 1970s, Levy tracked Dr Harvey to an office in Wichita, Kansas, and was shown those portions of Einstein's brain which had not been distributed. They were in a jar 'filed' in a old cider carton in the corner of the office.

According to the Soviet newspaper *Trud*, the brain of another worldfamous scientist, Dr Andrei Sakharov, was sent to the Soviet Academy's Neurological Institute after his death in 1989. Researchers there have been testing a theory that relates brain characteristics to a person's physical and psychological make-up. Other raw material for the study is said to include the brains of Lenin and Stalin.

The brain of Wyndham Lewis, the British writer and artist who died in 1957, is preserved, complete with the tumour.that killed him, in the Pathological Museum at the Westminster Hospital in London.

Jenkins' Ear

Actually this isn't still extant, as far as we know, but it is certainly one of the most curious ears in all history, not because of its shape or any physical characteristics, but because it gave its name to a war. The War of Jenkins' Ear (1739–1740) had its origins in the claim by Captain Robert Jenkins, Master of a brig called the *Rebecca*, that his ship had been raided by Spanish coastguards off Havana in 1731 and that in the skirmish that resulted, his ear had been severed by a certain Captain Fandino who was notorious for his cruelty. On his return to England, Jenkins' story inflamed anti-Spanish feeling, and the result, eventually, was not only the War of Jenkins' Ear, but also the War of the Spanish Succession (1740–1748).

Nose

No one had a more remarkable nose than the great Danish astronomer Tycho Brahe (1546–1601), but, once again, its fate is unknown to us. His first came to grief in a duel with a fellow student, brought about by an argument over who was the cleverer mathematician. But however noble Tycho's original nose had been (he came from an aristocratic family), the replacement literally outshone it, for it was made of gold.

Somewhere in China, there is a farmer with a most remarkable nose, according to a recent report by Reuters' man in Peking who wrote, 'A Chinese farmer whose nose was bitten off by a rat twenty-five years ago has regained his sense of smell after doctors built a replacement from a pig's ear.'

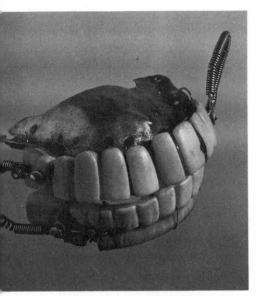

...s of fame: George Washington's teeth from the ...nsonian Institution in Washington, DC.

...r The head of St Oliver Plunket in its shrine in ...heda, County Louth, Eire. Plunket was martyred ...81 but not canonized until 1976.

Teeth

There is a veritable mountain of molars carefully preserved throughout the world.

George Washington, first President of the United States, commissioned some pretty exotic sets of dentures when his real teeth fell out. Some survived him to be presented to the Smithsonian Institution in Washington DC. Ivory from elephant's tusks was one material used, but other gnashers were made from the teeth of hippos, cows and possibly walrus. According to Dr Reidar Sognnaes, Dean of the University of California at Los Angeles School of Dentistry, (he identified the remains of Adolf Hitler and Martin Bormann by examining their gnashers), there is no truth in the legend that Washington's dentures were carved of wood. Dr Sognnaes said the President's teeth probably looked like wood because he enjoyed a glass of port, which stains ivory.

False teeth can also pick up radio signals under freak circumstances. A carpenter named George Dillard recently complained to the police near his home on Long Island, USA, that he could hear rock music in his head. Careful detective-work revealed that the metal in his dentures had tuned in to a radio station thirty miles away. All he had to do was take his teeth out at night to ensure a peaceful sleep.

One of the teeth of the Buddha is preserved in a gold-plated reliquary at the Temple of the Tooth at Kandy, Sri Lanka. It was brought to the island in the fourth century, hidden in the hair of a princess to prevent it from falling into hands of unbelievers. Today it is kept in the innermost sanctum of the temple, an object of veneration for Buddhists throughout the world. The Tooth Relic itself is rarely displayed or shown to visitors. Instead, the reliquary can be viewed: the tooth nestles at its very heart, enclosed in six other golden caskets.

Tongue

According to Father Herbert Thurston, the most authoritative of twentieth-century writers on religious phenomena, the tongues of several saints were found to be intact long after the rest of their bodies had decayed.

Thurston quotes the case of St Antony of Padua, whose tongue was housed in a special reliquary and was 'red, soft and entire' more than 400 years after his death. The tongue of Blessed Battista Varani met with less delicate treatment. 'The body had been found incorrupt thirty years after death,' writes Thurston.

A very arbitrary confessor ordered the nuns to rebury it between two planks and to water the earth thrown into the grave and beat it down, perhaps to blot out all memory of the place of burial. In 1593, some thirty-six years later, the grave was again opened and the bones of the *beata* were found, still fragrant, along with the dust of the body, while the tongue alone remained incorrupt, still moist and of a ruddy colour.

Face

Although the church at Mont de Cignes, France, in which the relics of St Fursey were kept, caught fire during the nineteenth century, the saint's face is said to have become imprinted upon the reliquary and thus, remarkably, survives to this day.

Jawbone

King Richard II's jawbone was stolen from Westminster Abbey by a mischievous schoolboy in 1776. It was not returned to the unhappy monarch's tomb until 1906.

Shoulder blade

Visitors to St Mary's Catholic Cathedral in Edinburgh can view a shoulder blade said to come from Scotland's patron saint, St Andrew. It was presented by Pope John Paul II.

RIGHT The heart of a thirteenth-century crusader is displayed in a glass case in the pillar of a church at Woodford in the English Midlands.

BELOW The Capua Leg was one of a wide range of prosthetics fashioned by the Etruscans in the centuries before the birth of Christ. They also turned out a fine line in dental bridgework in the form of teeth rivetted to gold bands.

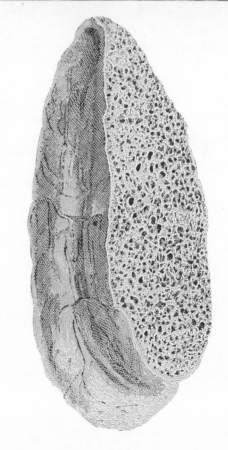

RIGHT A lung said to have belonged to the great English literary figure Dr Samuel Johnson.

Lung

One of the lungs of the great English lexicographer Dr Samuel Johnson was long thought to have been 'preserved' in an illustration for a medical textbook, *Morbid Anatomy* by Matthew Baillie, which was published in 1793. The illustrations, which were issued after the text, certainly included a fine picture of a lung.

Neither Baillie's book nor the engraving states definitely that the lung illustrated belonged to Dr Johnson. The evidence comes from a different source, a paper by G. J. Squibb published in the *London Medical Journal* of 1849 with the grandiose title *Last illness and post-mortem examination of Samuel Johnson, the lexicographer and moralist, with remarks*. Among the 'remarks' was a footnote stating that the illustration in Baillie's *Morbid Anatomy* showed Dr Johnson's lung after the dissection of the great man's body on 15 December 1784.

Yet modern experts are far from sure. One, Harold D. Attwood of the University of Melbourne, Australia, has expressed his doubts. Writing in the *Lancet* in 1985, he pointed out that the doctor who told Squibb that the lung in the picture was Johnson's had not been present at the autopsy and was therefore working from hearsay evidence. Attwood also questions whether the illustration shows signs of the emphysema from which Johnson suffered, or the symptoms of a different affliction. His conclusion? It cannot be Johnson's lung. If he is right, a mystery remains: whose lung *was* it that achieved a type of grisly immortality in Baillie's book?

Heart

The heart of a crusader, possibly Roger de Kirketon who died in 1280, is preserved in a glass-fronted niche in a pillar in the north aisle of St Mary's church, Woodford, Northamptonshire.

The heart of English poet and novelist Thomas Hardy (1840–1928) is buried in the graveyard of St Michael's church, Stinsford, Dorset, yet the ashes of the rest of his body lie in 'Poet's Corner' in London's Westminster Abbey.

Sir George Somers (1554–1610), founder of the town of St George's, Bermuda, left his heart abroad while the rest of his body was shipped back to Britain. It lies buried beneath a Bermudan garden. Sir George, incidentally, died of a 'surfeit of eating of a pig', so goodness knows what kind of state his heart was in.

Sadly, the heart of King Louis XIV of France is no longer extant. It was bought by a member of the Harcourt family from a grave robber during the French Revolution. The Harcourts kept it in a snuffbox, but one day one of them unwisely showed it to Dr William Buckland, the first Professor of Geology at Oxford University. Now Buckland had a great appetite for curious foods – among the more exotic dishes he sampled were crocodile and mole – and when he saw the embalmed heart he exclaimed, 'I have eaten many things, but never the heart of a king!' And before anyone could protest, Buckland popped it into his mouth and swallowed it.

Arm

One of the arms of St George, England's patron saint, is kept in a reliquary in St Mark's, Venice.

Hands

In 1987 the hands of General Perón (1895–1974), President of Argentina and husband of Evita, were stolen from his grave. A ransom note demanded five million pounds for their return. Sixty thousand people later turned up for a mass to mourn the theft. Said the current President, 'I think there are strange things happening in Argentina.'

Finger

In 1987 Chinese archaeologists reported the discovery of a hidden crypt in an ancient temple seventy miles from Xi'an, the home of the famous terracotta army. Inside was a heap of treasure, including a series of 'Chinese boxes' – four in all. An outer iron casket contained another of sandalwood, and the third was carved with rock crystal. In the fourth, of jade, lay a mildew-stained bone, which, according to an inscription on the outermost box, was one of the Buddha's finger bones, a relic apparently much revered by the rulers of the Tang dynasty (AD 618–906).

Bowels

The bowels of Eleanor of Castille, Queen of Edward I and mother of the first English Prince of Wales, are buried at Lincoln. After Eleanor's death in Nottinghamshire in 1290, the rest of her body was carried to London, where it is now buried in the Chapel of Edward the Confessor in Westminster Abbey. The journey left some of the most beautiful curiosities of the English landscape, the twelve stone crosses erected to mark the places at which the funeral cortege stopped. The most famous of all was London's Charing Cross, the last of the series. It was demolished in 1647, the stone being recycled as knife blades or paving in Whitehall. Only three Eleanor Crosses now survive: at Hardingstone and Geddington in Northamptonshire, and Waltham in Hertfordshire.

Genitals

Napoleon's penis was offered for sale at a London auction in 1969. The catalogue listed it as a 'small dried-up object, genteelly described as a mummified tendon taken from Napoleon's body during the post mortem'.

Legs

Thanks to grave robbers, William the Conqueror's left femur is all that remains of the great warrior in his tomb at the Abbey Church of St Etienne, Caen, France.

The Earl of Uxbridge's leg was the subject of a celebrated exchange at the Battle of Waterloo in 1815. 'By God, Sir, I have lost my leg,' the Earl is said to have cried at the height of the conflict. 'By God, Sir, so you have,' the Duke of Wellington is supposed to have replied. There are other versions attributing the sang-froid to His Lordship of Uxbridge. But there is no doubt that the leg was recovered and that it was buried in a small tomb paid for by local subscription. The tomb can still be found in the village of Waterloo in Belgium, albeit overgrown.

For artificial limbs it's hard to beat the Etruscans, a highly civilized people who flourished in central Italy from the eighth to the fifth centuries BC.

The Capua leg was their *pièce de résistance*. This remarkably sophisticated artificial limb was discovered in 1885 in a tomb thought to date from 300 BC on the site of the ancient city of Capua (near modern Naples). Its discoverers reported that they had found the skeleton of an amputee. Where its lower right leg should have been, was a wooden leg measuring 39.5 centimetres long (about 16 inches), sheathed in bronze. The limb obviously fitted below the wearer's knee and went down to the ankle: all trace of a foot, if there had ever been one, had disappeared.

For some reason, the leg ended up in London at the Royal College of Surgeons, where it was destroyed in a wartime bombing raid in 1941. Fortunately photographs survive, as well as an accurate copy made in 1910, now part of the London Science Museum's Wellcome Collection.

Knees

In the Philippines, kneecaps were in demand amongst members of a vigilante group, according to a report in November 1987. The vigilantes apparently dug them up from graves and hung them round their necks as a protection against enemy bullets.

Foot

What is claimed to be one of the feet of St Andrew is one of the treasures of Trier Cathedral in West Germany.

Toe

Feeling thirsty after all this reading? Well why not head for the Yukon and down a Sourtoe Cocktail? It's a grisly concoction invented by a larger-than-life character called Captain Dick Stevenson. The recipe is simple: immerse one human toe in a drink and swallow the liquor only.

The sourtoe saga began in 1973 when Stevenson found a pickled amputated toe in a cabin he had bought. The first tasting, with the toe immersed in a beer glass filled with champagne, took place in the Eldorado Hotel in Dawson City in the Yukon. The most important rule was, 'You can drink it fast, you can drink it slow – But the lips have gotta touch the toe.'

The original had been dunked in 725 drinks before it was accidentally swallowed by a miner. A replacement was soon provided by a woman from Alberta who had had a toe amputated thirteen years earlier. Since then, other amputees have come forward with their toes whenever Captain Stevenson has lost the cocktail's vital ingredient or had it stolen. Thousands of visitors to the Yukon have sampled the grisly delights of what must be the world's strangest drink – and survived.

Blood

The blood of saints has traditionally been revered. Today the most famous of such relics is the blood of St Januarius which is kept in two phials in the Cathedral at Naples in Italy. The blood is thought by many to have miraculous qualities, and crowds have traditionally gathered at three great festivals each year in the hope of seeing it liquify: a sign, the faithful believe, of good times to come. But not everyone is convinced by such claims. One theory recently advanced is that the blood is 'nothing more than a mixture of ox-bile and glauber salts'.

Less controversial blood, thought to have been shed more than 1,000 years ago by a Maya king in a dedication ceremony for a 'hieroglyphic staircase' – a type of elaborate inscription dating from the eighth century AD – was recently found during excavations at Copán, Honduras. It was caked on to the shell of a thorny oyster which had been buried in a pot, along with the instrument known to have been used by the ancient Maya for drawing blood during religious rituals.

Skin

A report from New Delhi in 1988 contained this curious information: 'A Hindu peeled off his own skin to make a pair of sandals, then travelled across India to offer them to his family deity.'

Since few people, presumably, are inspired to such heights of devotion, it may be comforting to know that substantial quantities of human skin are available in libraries, for accounts of nineteenth-century murders were often bound in the skin of the executed killer. One such tasteless volume is kept in the Bristol Public Record Office.

It dates from 1821, and contains an account of the dissection of one John Horwood by Richard Smith, the surgeon who carried it out, together with a transcript of Horwood's trial for the murder of a girl called Eliza Balsam.

An account of the dissection of a British murderer, John Horwood, bound in the executed killer's own skin. Before 1832, murderers' bodies were the only cadavers doctors and medical students were allowed to dissect, and they often provided macabre mementoes.

21

Polar peculiarities

The first explorers of the polar regions expected to find curiosities. And find them they did. For example, in the eighteenth century, when the naturalist Georg Wilhelm Steller visited what is now known as Bering Island in the north, he found four previously unrecorded sea-mammals: the sea otter, the sea-lion, the fur-seal and the strange, enormous sea-cow later named after him. The discovery was as timely as it was interesting: the explorers were suffering from starvation and only an immediate cull of the newly-classified creatures enabled them to live to tell their tale. Today, rich tourists can even take a trip through the once-elusive North-west passage, yet the frozen north still yields a rich harvest of the weird and wonderful.

Cold clam

In 1986 William Zinsmeister of Purdue University, Indiana, USA, announced that he had discovered a fossilised clam seventy-five million years old and four feet across. 'It would most probably have made one hell of a clam chowder,' he said.

The U-boat secret

A chance entry in a Second World War U-boat log, spotted some forty years after the end of hostilities, led to a curious discovery on the tip of Labrador, on Canada's north-east coast. It also brought the solution to a mystery which had long baffled historians: how did the Germans manage to track down so many ships in the North Atlantic in 1943 and attack them with such precision?

The entry, in the log of submarine U-537, referred to a secret journey it had undertaken. The U-boat had crossed the Atlantic and landed two scientists on the Canadian coast. Their mission was to set up a meteorological and direction-finding station.

From photographs taken at the time, a Canadian Defence Department historian, Dr Alec Douglas, was able to identify the landing-site as a stretch of the Labrador coast. Dr Douglas then travelled to the area with Franz Selinger, the man who had discovered the story, and, some twenty miles from the northernmost tip of Labrador, they found the remains of the automatic station which had enabled the U-boat fleet in the North Atlantic to strike with such deadly accuracy.

The pole of cold

The village of Oymyakon in north-eastern Siberia in the USSR shares, with the town of Verkhoyansk some 400 miles to the south-east, the dubious distinction of being the coldest inhabited place on earth. The temperature there has been known to sink as low as −68°C. Oymyakon's 4,000 inhabitants – fur farmers, trappers and reindeer herders – can take consolation in the fact that there is one place that is even colder: at the other Pole of Cold, in Antarctica, the temperature gets down to the minus seventies! No one, however, is unwise enough to try to live there.

Bears behind bars

Churchill, a town on the shores of Canada's Hudson Bay, boasts one of the world's strangest prisons – a penitentiary for polar bears.

The bears fall foul of the authorities in Churchill, which calls itself 'the polar bear capital of the world', when more than a thousand of them

The Verkhoyansk district of Siberia in the USSR boasts some of the coldest temperatures on earth, and a few hardy inhabitants who specialize in reindeer-herding and trapping on the shores of the Tompo River.

Surtsey, the volcanic island which burst to the surface of the sea off Iceland in 1963.

invade the town every autumn. They are hungry and irritable after the thin pickings of the arctic summer and scavenge what they can from the town's rubbish bins while they wait for the ice to form on the bay and the opportunity to hunt seals – their favourite food.

They end up in the slammer when they run amok: a wooden house can be reduced to matchwood by a bear determined to let nothing stand in its way in its search for food.

When the bay has frozen, the 'convicts' are released and are free to roam the ice in search of a good meal.

Instant island

The island of Surtsey appeared in the sea off Iceland as the result of a volcanic explosion in November 1963. Two years later, it measured some two-and-a-half square kilometres. While two other lava islands which appeared at the same time soon sank back beneath the ocean, Surtsey seems to be here to stay and plants are now growing there.

The ship beneath the ice

The wreck of the *Breadalbane*, a British ship launched in 1843, is the most northerly ever discovered. She sank in the 1850s during the search for Sir John Franklin's lost expedition, and lies off Beechey Island in the Canadian Arctic, almost 350 feet down. A layer of ice six feet thick covers the spot. Yet, remarkably, the *Breadalbane* has been located and photographed. First by side-scan sonar which in 1980 produced a spectral image of an astonishingly well-preserved ship, and then by a robot camera. Finally, a diver in a sophisticated diving suit, designed to withstand the iron-fisted Arctic cold, was able to explore the wreck. An early prize was the ship's wheel, preserved after more than a century beneath the sea, its spokes festooned with coral.

The ice billiard table

Probably the strangest billiard table ever constructed was the one devised by English polar explorer Richard Collinson to amuse his men while his expedition was wintering at Cambridge Bay, Victoria island, Canada, in 1852. Since there was of course no green baize or slate available, Collinson ingeniously made the best possible use of the available materials: the table itself was built of blocks of snow, the bumpers of stuffed walrus skin, and the surface was a glistening sheet of ice.

Polar post

In the frozen south, intrepid explorers and settlers have created curiosities. With commendable enterprise, New Zealand Post set up the world's southernmost post office – at Scott Base in Antarctica. In 1987, however, it was closed and its staff of three transferred home to New Zealand. Two rather unsurprising reasons were given for the office's demise: it cost too much to run and did too little business. But should you be desperate to send a card home, there are now post offices at other bases, including the Chilean air force's establishment at Teniente Marsh on King George Island in the South Shetlands.

Snow baby

The largest land organism native to Antarctica is a wingless fly less than 4 millimetres long. But larger creatures have been born amidst the snowy wastes. Emilio Marcos Palma, a boy born in January 1978 at the Argentinian Esperanza base in Graham Land, is the first person known to have been born on that continent. His mother was flown there specially during her pregnancy to achieve this 'first'. It is not known whether Emilio's birth significantly strengthened Argentina's territorial claims.

Can-tarctic curios

About 200 photographs taken by the first man to the South Pole, Roald Amundsen, on his successful expedition of 1911–12, turned up in 1986 – in an old Horlicks tin.

Other Antarctic curiosities also come in tin cans. The climate acts as a natural refrigerator, and supplies abandoned or not used by expeditions have often long outlasted the explorers who brought them to the continent. In 1956, for example, *The Times* reported that an American Antarctic expedition had docked in New Zealand with a cargo of 'leftovers' from South Pole attempts led by Captain Scott and Sir Ernest Shackleton in the early years of this century. Some of Scott's supplies remained in Antarctica, however, and in 1985 members of the 'In the Footsteps of Scott' expedition came across well-preserved clothing and provisions in a stone hut used by their hero's men at Cape Crozier.

So treasured are such trophies of human endeavour, that far to the north, amidst the dreaming spires of Oxford, a marmalade tin thought to have been taken south by Captain Scott is on show at Frank Cooper Ltd, makers of the famous Oxford marmalade.

Lost and found

In 1985 a 'For Sale' advertisement in a magazine led to the recovery of the wheel of Captain Scott's ship, *Discovery*, now berthed in the Scottish city of Dundee. The wheel had gone missing seventeen years earlier, but an eagle-eyed magazine reader spotted the advertisement and alerted the police. It turned out that the seller had bought it quite innocently in 1972. Soon the wheel was back in its rightful place – aboard *Discovery*.

n the files of Frank Cooper Ltd:
sold, the cook on Captain Scott's
o British Antarctic expedition,
ing rhubarb pies. Some of the
supplied by the Oxford firm was
d to be edible almost half a
tury later.

vgrange Tomb, Ireland. The
und, built of 200,000 stones,
tains this passage grave, precisely
ned by prehistoric skywatchers to
the first rays of the dawn sun at
midwinter solstice.

22

The first astronomers

The oldest intact building in the world, Newgrange Tomb in Ireland, at least 5,000 years old, was built specifically to trap, like a shaft of faerie gold, the light on one day each year, the sun's winter solstice.

Stonehenge, whatever its other purposes, was undoubtedly aligned to give that magnificent Midsummer Morning experience when the sun rises over the Heel Stone.

But it is now becoming clear that very ancient societies knew about not only the dramatic waxings and wanings of the sun and moon but also the most complex details of the intricate movements of the stars and planets – and that they built temples, observatories, marker monoliths, to foretell the appearances of the heavenly bodies in their exact places.

In many parts of the United States and Canada, there are not only rock carvings, which have been interpreted as recording celestial events like supernovas, but also spectacular and mysterious medicine wheels which have been associated with the Red Indians.

These medicine wheels feature in the ceremonies and rituals of the tribes in whose territory they lie, but it now seems that some are not only much older than tradition suggests but also that they provide astronomical data which can have been of great practical as well as religious use to the Indians.

Many of the medicine wheels are very spectacular, like the pattern above the Saskatchewan River at Medicine Hat, Alberta, in Canada. Each spoke of the wheel has its own little ring, with the spokes at different lengths.

The Bighorn Medicine Wheel, west of Sheridan in Wyoming, in the United States, is more symmetrical with twenty-eight spokes, a central hub and six exterior cairns. Twenty-eight spokes certainly suggest the lunar month, but researchers have in recent years described alignments with the sun and the stars as well.

One cairn is aligned across the centre with sunrise on Midsummer's Day, another is aligned with sunset on the same day – perhaps a safety device against a cloudy dawn in these northern latitudes. However, the other cairns give even more intriguing alignments around the summer solstice. They are aligned with the first moments that three of the brightest stars in the sky, Aldebaran, Rigel in Orion's belt, and Sirius make their appearance.

The first cairn indicates the line where Aldebaran would flash above the horizon briefly, just before dawn on the day of the summer solstice – the sun's herald on that one day of the year.

Another cairn indicates the line where Rigel duly appears exactly twenty-eight days later, and another where in another twenty-eight days Sirius, the brightest star of all, makes its first showing: the sign, perhaps, that, two lunar months after the solstice, winter is coming and it is time for migration.

The Bighorn Medicine Wheel may be no more than a few centuries old. But the Moose Mountain Wheel in Saskatchewan was almost certainly constructed more than 2,000 years ago. Carbon dating of its central cairn suggests it dates back as far as 600 BC.

Moose Mountain is much cruder in construction and has only five spokes, but again it is aligned on the summer solstice, and, extraordinarily, on the lines of the three great stars, Aldebaran, Rigel and Sirius, not as they now are at the summer solstice, for the constellations shift over the centuries, but as they were two millenia ago.

Around the same era, the Maya in South America were building vast temple observatories. At Uaxactún there were three temples in the east. From the top of one of the central pyramids they showed the line of both the summer and winter solstices and the spring and autumn equinoxes at dawn.

At another Maya ruin, Chichén Itzá, there is a two-storey cylindrical building with narrow horizontal slits. They exactly frame the extreme positions in which the planet Venus sets. Indeed, one of the few Mayan books which survived the orgies of burning by the Spaniards is the so-called *Dresden Codex*, which has a Venus Calendar stretching to more than 37,000 days and encompassing 65 of Venus's 584-day cycles.

There is a seven-kilometre-long Mayan solar temple at Copán in Honduras. But perhaps the most intriguing of the Central American sites is the complex at Oaxaca outside Mexico City.

Tropical people have always been interested in the days when the sun was at its zenith and casts no shadow at noon. Here at Oaxaca is a building constructed to permit a shaft of sunlight to enter down a narrow tube on just two days of the year – 8 May and 5 August – when the sun is at its zenith. Nearby is another building, deliberately aligned so that an observer could see where the bright star Capella rose as harbinger of the zenith sun.

There are ruins and buildings all over the world which have been studied in great detail by archaeologists, but the interest of astronomers in these remains is only recent. Already it seems that ancient peoples knew as much of astronomy as any modern man before the coming of the radio telescope – including being able to calculate the slow movement of the earth's polar axis which takes 26,000 years to complete.

23

A-maze-ing!

Join us on the winding path through the mazes of the world! But before we start, a note on some of the sights you'll miss – because many mazes and labyrinths have not survived into the present day.

The missing mazes

The first labyrinth known to us, the Labyrinth of Egypt, was destroyed in ancient times. The only consolation is that, from the descriptions that survive, it does not seem to have resembled modern mazes. Built on the shores of Lake Moeris in about 2000 BC, the Labyrinth of Egypt appears to have been a vast building containing the tombs of kings, and the lairs of sacred crocodiles.

There is no trace, either, of the most famous labyrinth of all: the one owned by King Minos on the island of Crete and in which Theseus is said to have slain the dreaded Minotaur. According to the legend, the pathways of the labyrinth were so intricate that Our Hero was only able to escape by following a trail of thread. Indeed, there is some doubt that the Cretan labyrinth ever did exist in the form of a maze. Some experts believe that it may have been a network of natural caverns or a dancing floor, or that the name simply denoted Minos's palace as a place where bulls were slaughtered with a double-headed axe called a 'labrys'.

A much more recent maze, now sadly destroyed, had perhaps the weirdest origins of all. It was a hedge maze begun in 1950 in the rectory garden at Wyck Rissington, a quiet village in the Cotswold hills of England. The inspiration for the work, which took six years to complete, came to its builder, Canon Harry Cheales, in a peculiar way. One night he had a dream in which he found himself looking out of one of the rectory windows, and in the garden below he could see people walking round a maze. A shadowy figure behind him was providing a sort of commentary upon the scene.

When the Rector awoke, he knew what he had to do. He must build the maze he had seen in the dream. Not surprisingly, the Wyck Rissington maze, with its winding pathways through the hedgerows, turned out to have an allegorical significance: it symbolised the journey of life. The cul-de-sacs encountered by visitors and the wrong turnings they took were to remind them of the obstacles that lie on the road to heaven.

The maze proved a popular local landmark, but Canon Cheales destroyed it when the rectory was sold, to prevent his inspired creation falling into secular hands.

Mazes have also fallen victim to progress. For example, the Science Museum in London now stands on the site of a maze constructed for Prince Albert, Queen Victoria's Consort.

The road to Jerusalem

Many of the world's oldest mazes are to be found in churches, in places as far apart as North Africa and Scandinavia, where they seem to have played a part in religious rituals. Those known as the 'Road to Jerusalem' were used by people who were unable to make a pilgrimage to the Holy Land. Instead, they made a symbolic journey, either by using a finger to trace the paths of a maze on the church wall, or by shuffling along a floor maze on their knees. The area in the centre was known as 'Jerusalem'. Other church mazes are thought to represent the journey of Christ from Pontius Pilate's house to Calvary.

Probably the oldest in existence is in Algeria, in the Church of Reparatus in Orléansville, which dates from the fourth century. The largest is in Chartres Cathedral in France, while a church at Telemark, Norway, boasts a more modest version painted on the wall. Italian examples, such as those in San Vitale Church, Ravenna, and Santa Maria-di-Trastavera, Rome, are richly ornamented with coloured marble, while in England, Ely Cathedral, Cambridgeshire, has an elegant maze beneath its west tower, an embellishment added during restoration work in the nineteenth century.

Treading the turf

The turf mazes of Old England were probably devoted to more secular pastimes, although the rules of the game usually played in them, known as the 'Game of Troy', are now lost.

Few of these turf mazes now survive, for nature is quick to reclaim shallow grooves in fields and commons, and many others have been ploughed up. One, at Boughton Green, Northamptonshire, never recovered from having training trenches dug through it during the First World War.

There are eight left: two in Hampshire, at Breamore and St Catherine's Hill, Winchster; a particularly fine example in the private garden of a farmhouse at Somerton, Oxfordshire; two in East Anglia, at Saffron Walden, Essex, and Hilton, Cambridgeshire; one in the Midlands at Wing, Leicestershire; and two in the North, at Brandsby, North Yorkshire, and Alkborough, Humberside. Alkborough also boasts three 'spin-off' mazes. One is in the church porch, another on a stained glass window behind the altar, and the third on the gravestone of one of the village's squires, who died in 1922.

Stone mazes

In Scandinavian countries, mazes made of boulders have been constructed in areas where grass or hedges do not easily grow. There are two on the island of Gotland in the Baltic and another at Tibble in south-east Sweden. Some were used by children for a game – with overtones of ancient fertility rites – in which boys raced each other down the curling pathways to reach a girl in the centre; others are thought to have been ritual sites which sailors visited for spiritual protection before embarking on a voyage.

Hedge mazes

Hedge mazes, perhaps the most familiar type of all, were originally commissioned, from the fourteenth century onwards, by the owners of great houses for the entertainment of their friends and guests. London's Hampton Court maze, planted in 1690, is a spectacular and much-copied example, although, by all accounts, a modest affair compared to those commissioned by some European royalty. For example, Louis XIV's maze

The pavement maze at Ely Cathedr
one of only two in Britain. It was la
out by the renowned architect Sir (
Gilbert Scott when he restored the
cathedral in 1870.

This tiny maze, set into the gravest
of a local squire who died in the 19
is one of four at Alkborough,
Lincolnshire. The others include a t
maze and a tiny labyrinth depicted
stained glass window in the village
church.

at Versailles, France, destroyed in 1775, had a fountain at every twist and turn with figures depicting characters from Aesop's Fables, while in Germany, the Prince of Anhalt's labyrinth included streams, tunnels and follies. The idea of mazes was even imported into China by European missionaries: the Emperor's Summer Palace at Yuan Ming Yuan boasted one in the eighteenth century.

In Britain there are still plenty of hedge mazes to visit, from Hazlehead Park in Aberdeen to Glendurgan in Cornwall, and new ones are being created: the world's largest was planted at Longleat House, Wiltshire, in 1978. The United States has some elaborate versions, notable amongst them the one grown from varieties of American holly at the old colonial city of Williamsburg, Virginia.

24

Loony loos

Think of an example of something essential to mankind, and you will find curiosities. Take the lavatory, for example . . .

Loos with a view

In Fulham, London, in 1985, a firm of architects acquired the lease of a Victorian public lavatory, after the local council had replaced it with a fully up-to-date 'super loo', and converted it into more than a thousand feet of fragrant office space for their own use. The architects also gave the place a charming new name: 'The Old Conveniences'.

At the town of Ellon in Aberdeenshire, Scotland, a haircutting business has been run for years from a converted Gents. The sign above the salon reminds customers of the place's past glories. It says: 'U're in Al's Barber Shop.'

Ooh-la-loo!

Only two of Paris's famous street urinals now survive. One, in the fourteenth *arrondissement*, was spared because it is so near a prison that the authorities feared a new, enclosed building might become a meeting place for criminals, and the other was in such a smart district – the sixteenth – that it had nostalgia value.

Listed loos

British interest in the preservation of the nation's heritage even extends to lavatories. Most notable of all is the three-seater outside privy owned by Mr Ernie Smith at Bishop's Tawton in Devon, which the Department of the Environment has listed Grade II.

A 1920s public toilet near Newcastle-upon-Tyne's Tyne Bridge, which was granted the same status, was described by an expert as 'one of the most sensitively designed buildings that you could ever find.'

Low-down from the loo

Contrary to popular belief, scientists do not spend all their time jetting off to conferences or delivering prestigious lectures. Some conduct their research in the very bowels – if you'll excuse the phrase – of ancient loos. Here are some of their findings.

The four tons or so of 'damp fibrous brown material' discovered in an undisturbed seventeenth-century privy at Oriel College, Oxford, revealed that the Provost and his wife ate a great deal of fruit, some of it imported: traces of wild strawberries, cherries, gooseberries, plums, figs, raspberries and grapes were found. Their diet also seems to have included spicy substances like black peppers, fennel and mustard.

Excavations at a Roman fort in Carlisle revealed that its occupants used old letters as well as rough cloth as toilet paper.

After excavating a medieval barrel latrine found in Worcester, a Birmingham University investigator's list of finds included bramble and grape seeds and the remains of plants which may have been used as medicines, such as black nightshade.

25

Curious capitals

Take the scenic route from Los Angeles to San Francisco, the legendary California Route 1 which at every twist, turn and hairpin bend seems to offer an even more spectacular view of the Pacific coast than you saw a mile back, and towards the end of a long day's driving you will come across the town of Castroville. Though the place is small, the claims it makes for itself are big. For Castroville is nothing less than the **artichoke** capital of the world. That's what the signs say on the way into town, and they'll sell you the spiky little *Cynara scolemmus*, or globe artichoke, by the sackful. Castroville, it turns out, is by no means the only town which has successfully managed to put itself on the map by proclaiming itself the world capital of the product or service in which it specialises.

Austin, Minnesota, is the world capital of **Spam**, the tinned luncheon meat that troops in the Second World War loved to hate and which, more recently, was the butt of a memorable *Monty Python* sketch. The name was conjured up by a local actor in the 1930s. In a witty reflection of the way the meat is processed, he simply compressed the words 'spiced ham' and won himself the hundred-dollar prize on offer from Spam's makers, George Hormel.

In July 1987 Austin held a four-day festival in honour of their contribution to world gastronomy, the fiftieth aniversary of the creation of Spam, and the successful sale of 4,000 million tins to an ever-hungry world. Among the more bizarre events on offer were an art show, in which Spam starred in every picture, and a firework display culminating in a fiery tableau of a Spam breakfast. And even when there is no major anniversary to celebrate, the competitive instincts of Spam-lovers are allowed free reign in the Texas Annual Spam Cook-Off: first prize, the Spamericas Cup – of course.

Even without Spam on the menu, Battle Creek, Michigan, calls itself 'the **breakfast** capital of the world', and to justify its title the town lays out a breakfast table each June that extends for four blocks, or half a mile.

Gilroy, California, proclaims itself to be the globe's **garlic** capital. At the town's annual Garlic Festival, garlic ice cream is top of the menu.

Rivalling garlic in its smelliness is the **ramp**, an onion-like plant that grows only in the Appalachians of West Virginia. Ramps are so deeply embedded in the culture of the area that a local newspaper is reported to have once impregnated its printing ink with their nostril-zonking scent. The world capital of this (fortunately) rare product is Richwood, West Virginia, which holds an annual ramps festival.

If you love magic, Colon, Michigan, is the place to visit in August. It's the **conjuring** capital of the world.

Go **bananas** with a piece of the one-ton banana pudding at the International Banana Festival held at Fulton, Kentucky and South Fulton, Tennessee each September. The two towns, the 'Banana Crossroads of the United States' and the 'Banana Capital of the World', are twinned and not only share a name but a desire to spread the word about the curved yellow fruit.

In Hannibal, Missouri, you'll find the Becky Thatcher Bookshop, the Tom 'n' Huck Motel, the Mark Twain Dinette and the Injun Joe Camp Ground. No prizes then for guessing that Hannibal is the **Huckleberry Finn and Tom Sawyer** capital of the world. Samuel Langhorne Clemens, who created the enduring characters under the pseudonym of Mark Twain, lived here as a boy, and his house is carefully preserved, next door to a museum dedicated to his memory. Among the memorabilia on display there are the great man's typewriter and a portrait bust carved from soap.

Perhaps the weirdest world capital of all is down in the Deep South of the USA at Salley, South Carolina. Salley claims to be the **Chitlin'** capital of the world. Chitlins, or chitterlings as the English call them, are defined by the *Oxford English Dictionary* as 'the smaller intestines of the pig,' but don't let that put you off Salley's Chitlin' Strut at which, each November, several tons of the frilly piggy portions are eagerly consumed.

But if there were one world capital above all others that we would like to visit it is Bishop, California. Bishop calls itself the **mule** capital of the world, and on its annual Mule Days the town organises an event that encapsulates the wild, whacky and ingenious thinking of smalltown America at play: a braying contest – for humans.

26

Oddball Oregon

In Oregon:

- there are more ghost towns, abandoned gold mines, and one-man cities – complete with mayor – than in the rest of America combined.

- stand the vast lava mountains of McKenzie where the astronauts came to practise for the moon. Nothing has grown here for 3,000 years.

- geology has gone wild. There is a one-mile-long natural tunnel through the lava.

- is Crack-in-the-Ground, where you can walk for two miles up to seventy feet below ground.

- lies the town of Gouge Eye, named after a famous brawl, and the town of Joseph where three men robbed the bank in 1902 and one of them subsequently got himself elected bank president.

- is the Jordan Valley where there are Basques who still speak Basque. It is the home of the world's most westerly pelota court.

- there are still buffalo herds.

- a whole area – towns, river, dam, is named after John Day, a Virginian who was known to be certifiably insane.

- the town of Westfall has a post office but no residents – not even the post master lives there.

- Fort Stevens is the only place on the mainland United States to have come under enemy fire in the Second World War. A Japanese submarine

ᴏᴠᴇ Oddball games in Oddball Oregon are played in the world's most westerly pelota court, built by ᴂque immigrants from Spain.

ᴏw Main Street in John Day, a town named after an insane settler from Virginia.

surfaced and shelled the old coastal fortification near Warrenton. The ancient guns at the fort lacked the range to reply. The submarine dived and slipped away with a unique distinction.

* is the place where the only casualties in the Second World War from an attack on the mainland United States occurred. Five people were killed by a bomb carried across the Pacific from Japan by a rice-paper balloon. In May 1945 the Reverend Archie Mitchell and his wife were out on a Sunday School picnic at Gearhart Mountain, near Bly, Oregon, when one of the children found the strange object. As they gathered round, it exploded, killing Mrs Mitchell, who was pregnant, and five of the children. More than forty years later, a Japanese-American professor tracked down some of the Japanese women who, as schoolgirls, had been taken from their classrooms in the last desperate months of the war and sent to a special plant. There they made the balloons, filled them with hydrogen, and attached the bombs, which were despatched when weather conditions were favourable. In September 1987 some of the women sent a thousand paper cranes to the Oregon families, 'seeking forgiveness and as a prayer for peace'.

27

Fakes or the real thing?

Archaeological journals thrive upon controversy. Their pages may look austere, but often, amidst the learned footnotes and the conventions of academic argument, passions run high. Never more so than when a find is thought to have been faked but forgery or hoax prove difficult to establish.

Mention any of the following cases where two or three archaeologists are gathered together, and the chances are that you will do best to stand well back and let the arguments rage.

Cave of controversy

Rouffignac is one of the many cave systems in the Dordogne area of France adorned with prehistoric art, the most famous being Lascaux a few miles away. One guidebook describes it as 'a pantheon of prehistory with 11 km of galleries and more than 200 rock carvings.' But how genuine are the pictures?

The late Professor Glyn Daniel of Cambridge University, an expert on the Dordogne caves, had serious doubts. He was unable to reconcile the date given for the discovery of the cave paintings – 26 June 1956 – with what he knew about the cave in the years that immediately preceded it. How was it, he wondered, that a frieze can be clearly seen in a photograph of Rouffignac published three years *before* the 1956 'discovery' and apparently taken more than *twenty years* before that? Furthermore, wrote Daniel in 1984, in the leading British journal *Antiquity*, of which he was Editor:

We are still waiting for an explanation of why Martel, the great French speleologist who knew Rouffignac well, the abbé Breuil, who visited it in 1915, and the abbé Glory, who visited the site in 1948 with Dr Koby of Bâle, made no mention of having seen any paintings or engravings.

Daniel also cites:

the testimony of Colonel Arthur Walmesley-White who visited Rouffignac with the Cambridge University Speleological Society in March 1939 – a group of keen, healthy, vigorous, sharp-eyed young men trained in geology and archaeology who had already spent a week visiting all the other painted and engraved caves in South West France. He says, 'We never saw any drawings or paintings and ... the owner didn't know of any.'

One possibility is that *maquisards* of the French Resistance, who used the caves as hiding-places during the Second World War, may have dabbled in a little pseudo-prehistoric art. Professor Daniel offered these thoughts:

[I] now think that there *may* have been some original authentic paintings and engravings improved and added to by maquisards. And yet, and yet, and this is the question we always come back to in discussion of Rouffignac with our French colleagues: if there were original authentic paintings why were they missed by Martel, Breuil, Glory, Koby and Severin Blanc?

A judgement only marginally less outspoken than that of another expert quoted by the sceptical professor: 'There are two styles represented at Rouffignac – one is a pastiche copy of other palaeolithic art, the other is *Babar l'Eléphant!*'

Authenticating the stone

Is the Stone of Scone that lies under the Coronation Chair in London's Westminster Abbey the same stone which was kept at the place where all the early kings of Scotland were crowned and was regarded by them as a sacred symbol of power?

Two rumours connected with the stone's travels have suggested it may not be. The first, some 700 years old, asserts that a fake stone was substituted for the real one when news reached Scone that King Edward

I of England, the 'Hammer of the Scots', was on his way to seize it in 1297. According to the legend, the stone was hidden for many centuries in the ruins of Dunsinane Castle, near Perth, before being moved, in the nineteenth century, to a nearby farm where it still lies.

The second rumour arose after the Stone of Scone was stolen from Westminster Abbey by Scottish nationalists in 1950. It was later returned. But whispers that a copy was substituted can still be heard.

Bone of contention

The 'Sherborne Bone' came to public attention soon after two new boys at the English public school, Sherborne, claimed to have discovered it in October 1911, and controversy about its true origins has surfaced regularly over the years.

The 'Bone' is, in fact, a small fragment, but its potential importance lies in the picture of a horse engraved upon it. The question the archaeologists have been trying to answer for the past three-quarters of a century is this: is the 'Sherborne Bone' a fake, the product of a schoolboy jape, or is it a rare and important example of prehistoric art?

The two finders were adamant that they had chanced upon the bone in some stony ground near the school, but their claims were countered by rumours that the whole affair had been staged to hoax the science master and that the bone had been modern – scavenged from the local rubbish dump.

The schoolboys and the experts originally involved are long dead, but the controversy continues. With successive academic papers, opinion about the authenticity of the bone seesaws. One test, for example, has shown that it is fossilised; nevertheless, an expert on the style of palaeolithic artists firmly pronounced the engraving to be fake. The Sherborne find, now in the possession of the Natural History Museum in London, has proved a bone of contention indeed.

The plate of brass

In the summer of 1936 a young man called Beryle Shinn was idly rolling some rocks down a hill overlooking San Francisco Bay when he noticed a piece of metal sticking out from underneath a rock. 'Just the thing to mend my car with,' he thought, and picked it up. He noticed that the

Is it a bird? Is it a reptile? [A] fake? *Archaeopteryx* from [the] Natural History Museum[,] London.

The Fuller Brooch from th[e] British Museum was once[ ]thought to be a fake, but [ ]experts have authenticate[d it as] a ninth-century masterpi[ece.]

metal seemed to be covered with writing, but he took it home and left if lying around for six months. It was then that one of his friends noticed either the word 'Drake' or a date, 1579 (accounts vary). Shinn was persuaded to show it to Herbert Bolton, Professor of History at the University of California.

Bolton was astounded. Shinn appeared to have found a relic which he had longed to discover: the brass plate which the English explorer Sir Francis Drake had erected to mark his visit to California in 1579. Drake's chaplain, Francis Fletcher, left this account:

> Before we went from thence, our generall caused to be set vp, a monument of our being there; as also of her maiesties, and successors right and title to that kingdome, namely a plate of brasse, fast nailed to a great and firme post . . .

Professor Bolton believed the brass plate found by Shinn to be genuine, and announced in 1937 that 'the authenticity of the tablet seems to me beyond all reasonable doubt'.

But was it? True, a panel of experts which tested the plate in 1938 declared, 'It is our opinion that the brass plate examined by us is the genuine Drake Plate . . .', but other experts remained unconvinced. Some worried about the crude appearance of the plate; 'a clumsy botch,' one called it, yet Drake had taken skilled craftsmen on his expedition. Others thought that the spelling was modern. Yet another, suggested that the plate contained more zinc than other brasses of its supposed period.

In the 1970s a new investigation was ordered by the Bancroft Library of the University of California, Berkeley. Its findings, published in 1977, cast doubt not only upon the 1930s test results but also upon Profesor Bolton's acceptance of the plate as genuine.

A whole battery of the most up-to-date techniques was used, and the experts' conclusions brought no comfort to those who still believed that the plate was the very one posted by Sir Francis Drake in 1579. For example, two separate laboratories confirmed that the plate contained more zinc than is found in brasses known to have been made before 1600, and less lead. A painstaking microscopic examination revealed that the plate had been made by a rolling process, not used until after Drake's time: sixteenth-century brass plates were invariably hammered out. Furthermore, the edge of the plate showed tell-tale signs of having been cut with a guillotine and not with a chisel, the standard Elizabethan tool for the job.

Despite its thoroughness, this latest report leaves many questions unanswered. Not least these: if the Plate of Brass was a hoax, who perpetrated it and why? And does the real one still lie undetected somewhere on the coast of California?

Archaeopteryx gets the bird

Archaeopteryx has always been held to be one of the most important fossils ever discovered, for it appears to be an evolutionary 'missing link', halfway between a reptile and a bird. One specimen, discovered in a Bavarian quarry in 1861, is owned by the Natural History Museum in London; another, found at the same location in 1877, is now in a museum in Berlin.

In 1985, however, British scientist Sir Fred Hoyle and five colleagues claimed that both fossils were fake. A detailed photographic examination of the 1861 *Archaeopteryx*, they said, had led them to conclude that the forger had been Karl Häeberlein, the Bavarian doctor who had sold it to the Natural History Museum in the 1860s. Their main allegation was that Häeberlein had faked the creature's feathers by first smearing a paste of crushed limestone around a perfectly genuine reptile fossil and then pressing chicken feathers into it to give the reptile 'wings'. The new photographs, Hoyle argued, were so fine that the chewing-gum-like remains of the cement could still be seen.

The London guardians of *Archaeopteryx* were incensed. Said one, 'We think the suggestion that it's a fake is a load of codswallop.' The museum drew up a detailed rebuttal of the Hoyle team's claims and cited the discovery of three more specimens since 1950 as evidence against forgery. The intensity of the row, according to one newspaper report, 'would not have disgraced a Glasgow pub at closing time'.

By 1987, however, the boiling pot of controversy had simmered down. One beneficial effect of the row, as far as the general public was concerned, was that the Natural History Museum mounted an excellent special display of *Archaeopteryx* for everyone to enjoy.

Warning

Finally, the case of the Fuller Brooch is a reminder that it is never easy – or wise – to state that an object purporting to be ancient is definitely fake. The brooch, said to date from the ninth century, had long been dismissed as a forgery, until it was re-examined by modern experts – and authenticated. Now it is an important and valuable exhibit in the British Museum, London.

28

Stonehenge – the fakes!

You might think that for the world to have one Stonehenge was enough. Yet to some enterprising people, the urge to construct their own version of Stonehenge has proved irresistible.

No prizes for guessing that the most eccentric and spectacular fakehenges are in North America. At **Maryhill**, in the USA's **Washington State**, stands an imposing concretehenge erected in the 1920s by a railroad tycoon, Sam Hill, as a memorial to local men who died in the First World War. Sam had high standards. No lugging of knobbly sarsen stones for him and his labourers: unlike its tumbledown inspiration on Salisbury Plain, the Maryhill concretehenge is immaculate, with not a block out of place. It stands in splendid isolation above the Columbia River. Not surprisingly, Sam Hill himself chose to be buried there, within sight of his extraordinary monument.

At **Rolla, Missouri**, the University of Missouri boasts a prize-winning modern interpretation of the monument, designed to recreate the circle's supposed astronomical alignments rather than its every architectural detail. At the winter or summer solstice, sunset can be viewed through a gap in one of the trilithons.

Both these splendid fakehenges, however, are eclipsed as oddities by 'Autohenge' and 'Carhenge'. As its name suggests, 'Carhenge' at **Alliance, Nebraska**, was built by a Mr James Reinders from old vehicles: a pickup truck, an ambulance and twenty cars. 'Autohenge', commissioned by the Chrysler car company for an advertisement, was constructed by sculptor Bill Lishman at **Blackstock, Ontario**. A truly remarkable work of art, closely conforming to the measurements of the original Stonehenge, 'Autohenge' appeared on the cover of a folder which accompanied an exhibition called *Visions of Stonehenge* held in Southampton, England, in 1987. At first glance, few people can have realised that they were not looking at a photograph of the real thing.

British replicas have proved less remarkable. There is one at **Ilton**, near Masham, Yorkshire, designed in the early ninetenth century by an eccentric called William Danby of Swintonhall, with the praiseworthy aim of providing work for the unemployed.

A tiny concretehenge was run up by a **Southampton** man called William Burroughs Hill, but it was destroyed in the Second World War. At **Weston Rhyn, Shropshire**, a fakehenge modelled on Stonehenge's 'rival', Avebury, was erected in the early years of the nineteenth century by a landowner who wished to improve the scenery.

Striking though these latter-day henges undoubtedly are, none of them can compare with the genuine article in at least one vital respect. They do not evoke, as Stonehenge or Avebury or Arbor Low, the 'Stonehenge of the North', evoke, a sense of wonder at the achievements of the people of ancient times who must have laboured long years – perhaps for most of a lifetime – to erect the monuments, curiosities in themselves, that we admire today.

29

Number geniuses

In the bleak and regimented world of Stalin's Moscow, there was one comfortable book-lined apartment, redolent of the relaxed and academic world of Oxford or Cambridge, to which came some of the strangest geniuses on earth. For this was the home of Professor Luria, whose interest in the workings of the human brain had led him to study people with phenomenal powers of memory or calculation.

Luria's most famous case was the man he called 'S'. S. could remember an almost infinite list of anything he heard, but especially numbers. Eventually, he became an entertainer, performing nightly round the small theatres in the Moscow region. He would get the audience to call out anything they liked and then would recall the list of items immaculately. But his star turn was when he would go round the whole audience asking them to shout out any number up to five digits long. Then, when he had heard perhaps from five hundred people, he would go back round the audience repeating each individual's number. Occasionally, if he got one wrong, he would, on being challenged, go back and correct himself.

Luria discovered that what S. was doing in his mind – there was no trickery about it – was selecting some familiar place – a street in his home town – and mentally walking down that street, placing each number as it was called out in one doorway or another. Hence his ability, if he made a mistake, to go back and retrieve the right number.

S. had, however, one problem. He found it very hard to forget. Erasing the numbers from the previous night's performance was a great strain, such that he had to give up his performances. And not long after, he died.

For many years doctors around the world have been interested in the talents of apparently mad or mentally deficient people to perform prodigious feats.

In the last century, there was the ten-year-old Vermont boy Truman Henry Safford. The Reverend H. W. Adams, an amateur scientist, studied him. He asked him to multiply the number 365,365,365,365,365,365 by itself.

The Reverend Adams wrote:

He flew about the room like a top, pulled his pantaloons over the tops of his boots, bit his hands, rolled his eyes in his sockets, sometimes smiling and talking, and then seeming to be in agony, until, in not more than one minute, said he: '133,491,850,208, 566,925,016,658,299,941,583,225.'

In the eighteenth century, there was the Englishman Jedediah Buxton who could apparently understand no basic arithmetic but could conduct complex astronomical calculations.

In the 1930s, two doctors, Snyder and Rife, reported a patient who, when asked to say how many grains of corn would be on the last square of a chess board if you started with one on the first and doubled the number on each subsequent square up to the final sixty-fourth, was able to give the right answer to this famously difficult problem in forty-five seconds. It is 18,466,734,709,551,616.

In recent times, the most celebrated strange savants have been a pair of identical twins born in 1939 and hospitalised at Letchworth Village Institution in New York State, on the grounds that they were mentally deficient.

When they were fourteen, Dr William Horwitz noticed that they seemed to have an unusual facility with birthday dates. He started giving them tests which developed into an intense examination course.

The twins, bespectacled and hardly able to communicate in any normal way, could instantly identify the years, way into the future, when any given date would fall on a Sunday. They could take any date up to the year AD 6000 or more and identify what day it would be, allowing for leap years and all the complexities of the century's end. They could do the same backwards, apparently even compensating for the switch from the Julian to the Gregorian calendar two centuries ago.

But after a whole year of tests, Dr Horowitz could arrive at no understanding of how the twins worked out their calculations. All they would say to him was: 'It's in my head.'

т An English
ge savant, J. H.
n, the so-called
us of Earlswood
um,' built this ten-
nodel of a ship,
to the smallest
l, from his own
s, and even made a
al machine to
ace the million pins
red to assemble it.

w St Michan's
ch, Dublin, Eire,
s a macabre tourist
ction: visitors can
e hands with the
ery corpses in the

30

Grave matters

Sadly, the fate of one's mortal remains is often beyond one's control. What would the Irish Crusader have thought, had he known that his leathery hand would still be available for shaking 700 years later by every passer-by in the crypt of St Michan's Church, Dublin – the whole corpse apparently miraculously conserved by the dry atmosphere in the ecclesiastical basement?

Even when the cremation has turned ashes to ashes, misadventure can still come along. D. H. Lawrence's lover, Frieda, having once inadvertently left his ashes on a Mexican railway platform while hastening to the embraces of her Italian *amour* Angelo Ravagli, and then having the urn stolen by a rival, finally, on retrieving them, had them shovelled into a concrete mixer and included in the slab which was being made for her new mantelpiece.

Such as remained of Admiral Nelson's already depleted body was, of course, brought home in a rum barrel after his death at the Battle of Trafalgar in 1805 – the Admiralty preferring it pickled rather than putrified for a suitably honorific burial in St Paul's Cathedral.

The American government had a much more searching task when they discovered that the hero of the American revolution, John Paul Jones, had been mislaid in Paris for 113 years owing to a bureaucratic error.

Jones, the scourge of the British Navy during the revolutionary war, had continued his career in the Russian Navy. He finally died in Paris and the grateful Americans paid for his body to be embalmed with a view to its being shipped home across the Atlantic. Then he was forgotten and the French buried their embarrassment in a public cemetery. The twentieth century had arrived before the United States government thought to enquire further. It turned out that the cemetery had long been enveloped

in commercial development. Full of belated ardour, the Americans unearthed an old map of the cemetery showing the approximate location
of graves. Next, they employed a squad of miners who set out from
the nearest accessible point to tunnel hundreds of feet round drains,
cellars and foundations towards the reputed spot of Jones's coffin.

Eventually, after disturbing the rest of several deceased Frenchmen, they
found a lead casket with the initials J.P.J. on the lid. The body was
remarkably well preserved by the embalming, with the hands and feet
wrapped in metal. The coffin lid had pressed down on the Admiral's nose,
but otherwise he was like his portraits to the life. He was duly escorted
home in triumph to the US Naval College at Annapolis, Maryland, where
he now resides.

Over the centuries the disposal of bodies has inspired all manner of
eccentricities and curiosities.

Ashes to ashes

D. H. Lawrence may not have intended his lover's mantelpiece to be his
last resting-place, but others have requested that their ashes should be
scattered in places which meant much to them during their lives. That is
why the ashes of golfer Ollie Small are somewhere in the sand of the
fourth-hole bunker at the Stanford University golf course in California.

Frank Goldsworthy of Orlando, Florida, left instructions after his death
in 1982 that he wished to have his ashes scattered in the Atlantic. His
reason was rather touching: he had left his father aboard the ill-fated
Titanic when she sank in 1912.

Corpses are less portable and not so easy to dispose of as ashes – which
can lead to all kinds of complications. In 1985 two American states were
locked in dispute over the remains of the celebrated architect Frank
Lloyd Wright. Wright was originally buried at Spring Green, Wisconsin,
in 1959. Worried officials exhumed him soon afterwards because they
were worried that his last wish – to face his home – had not been carried
out. They turned him round and the great master of modern architecture
lay at peace until the death of his wife in 1985. She had requested that
his body should be dug up, cremated and moved to Scottsdale, Arizona,
where she wanted to be buried. She got her way.

Odd coffins

The Tenth Duke of Hamilton, who died in 1852, commissioned a huge and expensive mausoleum at Hamilton Palace, Lanarkshire, Scotland. His tomb was to be its centrepiece – an Egyptian sarcophagus which cost him the then vast sum of £11,000. The problem was that the Egyptian for whom the sarcophagus had originally been designed was somewhat smaller than His Grace, and the Duke's feet had therefore to be cut off and interred separately before the funeral could be completed.

Millionairess Sandra West of San Antonio, Texas, who died in 1977, chose a real status symbol as her coffin. She was buried in her nightdress, sitting in the front seat of her beloved blue Ferrari. To deter graverobbers, the car was encased in concrete.

In 1981, Dr David Stry, the owner of a Mexican health farm, made it known that when he died he wished to continue – from beyond the grave – the anti-smoking stance that he had maintained in life. He therefore asked his executors to ensure he would be buried in the non-smoking section of the cemetery – in a flip-top coffin.

What they took with them

'You can't take it with you,' is, of course, basically true, but many people are buried with a much-loved possession or in their favourite clothes.

Film star Bella Lugosi was buried in the cape that he wore in his Count Dracula role.

Poet Robert Graves was interred in the hilltop graveyard at Deya, Majorca, with his famous black hat.

Film star Humphrey Bogart's coffin contains a small whistle. Inscribed on it is a line from the first film in which Bogie and his widow Lauren Bacall starred together: 'If you need anything, just whistle.'

In 1986 Oxford printer Don Parchment was buried wearing his colourful Hawaiian shirt.

According to *Ask Sir James*, Michaela Reid's fascinating biography of her husband's grandfather, Sir James Reid, Queen Victoria left instructions that 'rings, chains, bracelets, lockets, photographs, shawls, handkerchiefs, casts of hands – all souvenirs from her life – early, middle and late' should be placed in her coffin. 'No friend or servant was forgotten, and each member of her family was remembered.' Sir James was Queen Victoria's doctor, and, after her death in 1901, her body was in his care until her

ven in death, poet Robert Graves refused to be parted from his famous black hat. It is buried with him.

coffin was sealed. Of the mementos of her servants, pride of place was accorded to those of her faithful Scottish ghillie, John Brown. Sir James described how he 'put in the Queen's left hand the photo of Brown and his hair in a case (according to her private instructions), which I wrapped in tissue paper...'

King Edward I of England was interred in fitting regal finery in 1307. When his tomb in London's Westminster Abbey was opened in the eighteenth century, the King was found to be dressed in magnificent robes. He was also wearing a gold crown and held a copper gilt sceptre in his hand.

Loony tombs

Pandering to the whims of the dear departed reached new heights when Mr Henry Trigg of Stevenage, Hertfordshire, died in 1724. He was so afraid of the body-snatchers prevalent in England at the time that he asked his brother to put his coffin up amongst the rafters of their barn, well out of the reach of anyone who might want to make off with his corpse. His brother did as he was asked, and the coffin stayed up in the roof for a century or so, before being replaced by a new model. This is still there, although the bones of Henry Trigg himself are no longer in it. It is not, however, thought that the body-snatchers got him in the end.

The remains of Queen Boadicea, Queen of the English Iceni tribe, who died in AD 60, are said to lie somewhere beneath Platform 10 of King's Cross railway station in London.

Some of the world's weirder tombs house the remains of animals. For example, in 1984 in Jamu, Kashmir, a mausoleum was commissioned by local Hindus to honour the head of a sacred cow, allegedly killed by Sikh extremists.

Memorable memorials

If you want serenity, visit an English graveyard; for architectural splendour there is nothing to beat a French cemetery; and for sheer wackiness, the Americans, as always, reign supreme.

When Ray Tse was killed in a car crash in 1980, his brother David, a New York businessman, decided to give him the gravestone he would have wanted: a seventeen-foot-long granite replica of a Mercedes-Benz 240-D,

The touching grave of Tiddles
[ca]t whose nine lives ended in the
[beautifu]l churchyard at Fairford,
[Glouce]stershire.

A memorial to 'the Old Fish'
[erected] after the death, in 1855,
[of a pe]t trout kept by William
[Keyte o]f Blockley, Gloucestershire.

IN MEMORY
OF THE
OLD FISH

UNDER THE SOIL
THE OLD FISH DO LIE
90 YEARS HE LIVED
AND THEN DID DIE
HE WAS SO TAME
YOU UNDERSTAND
HE WOULD COME AND
EAT OUT OF OUR HAND
DIED April the 20th 1855
Aged 20 YEARS

built from real Mercedes blueprints. The dead man's name is displayed on the front number plate.

Lyndon L. Colegrove of Kinderhook, Illinois, designed his gravestone in advance. It immortalises his favourite sport – golf. Thus, on one side, there is a huge golf ball on its tee; on the other, a bag of clubs, ready for use on the celestial course.

Two parking meters flank the grave of Archie Arnold at Fort Wayne, Texas. Each displays the simple message, all too familiar to motorists: 'Expired'.

But for touching memorials, the British are unequalled. Especially when they tell of cherished pets.

At Fairford in Gloucestershire, in a graveyard, stands an effigy of Tiddles the cat commemorating the faithful service of the church's most regular visitor, a moggie who died in 1980. In the same county, a plaque on the wall of Fish Cottage at Blockley is dedicated to the memory of 'the Old Fish', pet of a certain Mr William Keyte. Mr Keyte's son erected the plaque and included this affectionate piscine epitaph:

> Under the soil the old fish do lie,
> Twenty years he lived, and then did die.
> He was so tame, you understand,
> He would come and eat out of our hand.

Singular cemeteries

One of America's strangest burial plots is the Showmen's Rest at Woodlawn Cemetery, Forest Park, in south-west Chicago. It is marked by large sculpted elephants. As the name suggests, circus people are buried there, including about sixty of the victims of a rail crash in 1918, members of the Hagenbeck-Wallace touring circus. Many of the commemorative stones show the difficulty experienced by the rescue services in identifying the dead: one is simply marked '4 Horse Driver', another 'Unknown Female No. 43'. The circus fat man was accommodated in a double grave. The crash inspired a charmingly sentimental epitaph by Lydia M. D. O'Neil:

> Beneath the wider canvas of the sky,
>   With filmy ropes drawn taut from star to star,
> Play on, while soundless centuries go by!
>   We may not watch and wonder from afar,
> But we shall know that unto you 'twas given
> To play to all the lonely babes in heaven –

Gold star-dust for the spangles on your gowns,
Dear dancing-ladies and beloved clowns!

The State of Illinois boasts another peculiar graveyard, in the town of Carlock. Here your final resting-place is often decided by your political affiliations. Democrats are buried in the Woodford County Cemetery, Republicans in the McLean County Cemetery. The segregation apparently began after the death of Abraham Carlock, a descendant of the town's founder. His gravestone was inscribed, 'Here Sleeps the old Democrat.' The Town's Republicans were not pleased, and sought to rest in peace elsewhere.

Bonheur Memorial Park, near Baltimore, Maryland, is a shrine to Americans' love of their pets and the last resting-place of many much-loved creatures, including an elephant from the local zoo. Humans can also be buried there – with their pets if they wish.

❧ · ❧

31

That sinking feeling

Since there is more sea on this planet than dry land, it will not surprise you to learn that all kinds of weird and wonderful curiosities lie underwater.

Titanic curiosities

The remains of the *Titanic*, the 'unsinkable' liner which, nevertheless, sank on her maiden voyage on 15 April 1912, constitute the greatest underwater curiosity of all. They were found off the Newfoundland coast on 1 September 1985 by a joint US-French expedition. The liner herself has been so well preserved by the icy Atlantic waters that even the most fragile of the passengers' possessions have survived – a dollar bill, for example.

Among the relics that made it to dry land soon after the disaster are a deck-chair from the First Class section. It was found floating on the surface by a clergyman entrusted with the grisly task of recovering some of the bodies of those who drowned – more than 1,500. It is now in the Maritime Museum of the Atlantic at Halifax, Nova Scotia.

Even more evocative is the pocket watch which once belonged to a Swedish victim. Its hands show that it stopped at 2.34 a.m.: fourteen minutes after the ship finally went down. It was on show in Stockholm in April 1987 on the seventy-fifth anniversary of the sinking.

In London, the anniversary was marked by an auction of *Titanic* memorabilia in the ballroom of the Park Lane Hotel. One of the lots was probably one of the most curious ever to come under the hammer. This

168

was lot 23, described in the catalogue as 'THE GUN METAL HYDRAULIC STEERING TELEMOTOR, from the Captain's Navigating Bridge of the *S.S. Titanic*, with helm indicator, hand pumps, cocks and safety valves, *lacking teak steering wheel* – 122 cm high.' There was one small problem. The telemotor had not been salvaged. Any purchaser, therefore, would only have to stump up five per cent of his winning bid in the meantime. The lot went to the auctioneer for £70,000.

The auction also contained probably one of the creepiest letters ever written. It was from W. T. Stead to R. Penny of Bristol. Stead was a journalist and psychical researcher. Penny was an astrologer. Penny had written to Stead urging him not to travel on the *Titanic*. Stead's reply, sent the day before he sailed, reads:

Dear Mr Penny,
Thank you very much for your kind letter which reaches me just as I am starting for America. I sincerely hope that none of the misfortunes which you seem to think may happen to myself or my wife will happen, but I will keep your letter and will write to you when I come back.
I am,
yours truly
W. T. Stead

Some *Titanic* curiosities never made it on board. One was a chamber pot, delivered too late for the maiden voyage, which eventually came into the possession of the President of the Marine Archaeological Society. Then there was what the catalogue of a 1988 *Titantic* ephemera auction described as 'A silver-plated cake fork by Elkington with the White Star Line burgee, which was 'reputedly removed from the ship prior to sailing by a steward.' Another 'survivor' was a bench which was apparently taken off the ship at Southampton to make room for some other piece of equipment.

Two treasures which went down with the ship: the De Beer diamonds, valued in 1912 at a staggering £5 million, and a copy of the *Rubáiyát of Omar Khayyám* adorned with 100 square feet of gold leaf and 1,051 semi-precious stones. It had taken craftsmen in London two years to produce. Another weird lost cargo was a consignment of palms *en route* from an English nursery to Philadelphia.

The bronze steering telemotor from the *Titanic*, photographed on the sea bed by Dr Robert Ballard's expedition to the wreck. Enterprising auctioneers offered it for sale in London, although there seems little prospect of its ever being recovered from the deep.

Archaeologist Stuart Bacon leans on the tombstone of John Easey, the last survivor of the medieval lost town of Dunwich. There are fears that John Easey's remains will soon follow those of his fellow townspeople into the encroaching sea.

DeLorean's salmon traps

The dies which once stamped out the bodies of John DeLorean's ill-fated stainless-steel cars finished up as anchors for salmon traps 100 feet down in the Atlantic off County Galway, Eire. The dies, broken up into twelve five-ton sections were bought by fish farmer Ciaran Crummey from a Cork scrap dealer. Mr DeLorean reportedly thought it 'unusual you'd use $12 million of important body dies to weigh down fishing nets'.

Plants with a past

'Stromatolites', plants which helped create the Earth's supply of oxygen, still flourish beneath the sea off the Bahamas. The six-foot 'living fossils', well-known to scuba divers because of their strange appearance – they look like the walls of sunken cities – were identified by scientists in 1986.

The scuttled fleet

A few of the ships of the German Kaiser's Grand Fleet, scuttled at Scapa Flow in the Orkney Islands in June 1919, remain unsalvaged beneath the water. The battleship *König* is one 'survivor'. Over the years, the salvage rights have been sold to scrap dealers.

The village under the sea

A single tombstone on a Suffolk shore is the last remnant of Dunwich, a city which, before it was washed into the sea, was the capital of East Anglia and one of England's most prosperous towns. That was back in the Middle Ages, before a storm in 1347 destroyed 400 houses and began the process of decay which culminated in the collapse of Dunwich's last church, All Saints, in 1919.

Now the gravestone of John Easey clings precariously to dry land, and the great town has passed into legend. Do the church bells of Dunwich still toll beneath the waves? Local people claim they hear them, chiming a tune that sings of the impermanence of the works of man.

Lost leather

A chapter of accidents identified the strange treasure hidden in the wreck of the *Catherina von Flensburg*, a brigantine which sank in Plymouth Sound in 1786. First, divers from a local sub-aqua club came across the ship by accident when they were searching for another wreck. Then no one realised the rarity or value of the rolls of leather found, perfectly preserved, in her hold. That took the expertise of a top London shoemaker who was shown a salvaged roll while on a visit to Dallas, Texas. He identified it as Russia Leather, one of the greatest examples of the tanner's art, and a real rarity in the twentieth century, for the tanning formula was lost in the first Russian revolution in 1905.

The expert was able to acquire enough Russia Leather to make several pairs of shoes, including one for the Prince of Wales. And so great was the interest from prospective buyers that a lottery was held to determine who should have the privilege of paying £1,250 for a piece of shoemaking history.

Guy Garfit of a top London shoemaking company examines footwear made of the rarest material, Russia leather, salvaged from a shipwreck in Plymouth Sound.

The skeleton of a monster from the depths of Loch Ness. Not *the* fabled humped creature, however, but a Wellington bomber shot down in the Second World War.

32

Loch Ness – curious enough without the monster

If the Loch Ness Monster were ever found, the great Scottish lake would undoubtedly be assured of becoming the world's capital of curiosities. But since Nessie's hunters have persistently failed to prove she is anything more than a myth, let's concentrate instead upon some Loch Ness curiosities which have definitely existed.

The bomber on the bottom

One concrete result of the Loch Ness searches was the location, and recovery in 1985, of an RAF Wellington bomber which crashed into the water on a wartime training flight. After being raised from the depths of the loch, R-Robert was removed to the Brooklands Museum at Weybridge, Surrey, for restoration.

Whisky in water

Also in 1985, two schoolboys discovered a chest in the Loch. In it was a letter which explained that the chest had been hidden in 1969 as part of a treasure hunt organised by a whisky firm. But where was the prize – twelve bottles of 'the water of life' – which had been hidden in the chest? The schoolboys and the company were mystified – until a student from Bristol University revealed that on an earlier occasion he and nine other amateur divers had stopped at Loch Ness while on a trip to Scapa Flow,

Orkney, and had come across the chest during a dive off Torr Point near Dores. They had not noticed the letter explaining why the 'treasure' had been put there, the student claimed, so they had divided up the 'spoils' and carefully put the chest back into the loch without telling anyone.

Weapons, a body, and a famous boat

In 1969 a six-man submarine, owned by the British shipbuilders Vickers, located old weapons in Urquhart Bay. The investigators concluded that they had probably been discarded after Bonnie Prince Charlie's defeat in the uprising of 1745.

In 1932, Mrs Hambro, wife of a leading banker, disappeared after a boating accident. Her body was never recovered; nor was the valuable jewellery she was said to have been wearing.

Somewhere in the depths of the loch may lie fragments of the boat in which Sir John Cobb was killed while attempting to break the world water-speed record in September 1952. Eyewitnesses said that *Crusader* shot into the air and broke up after hitting the wake left by one of Cobb's guide boats.

The monster revealed

After our sceptical remarks at the beginning of this section, you will, no doubt, be surprised to hear that we believe there definitely *is* a monster somewhere in Loch Ness!

But don't get too excited, for it was a film prop used by Billy Wilder in his film *The Private Life of Sherlock Holmes*. After its starring role, the 'monster' sank and was abandoned.

33

Genuine fakes

Forgers, fakers and hoaxers are never idle. Whole books have been written about their skills and some of their most famous artefacts. Museums have even been dedicated to them. There is one in Paris, for example, in an eighteenth-century house – built, appropriately, in 1900! In 1990 London's British Museum devoted a major exhibition to the subject. So here are just a few fakes which have caught our eye. The ones we like best are those that make us chuckle. None more so than:

The Mullsjö runes

Runes are mysterious symbols used as a form of writing, much used in Scandinavia until round about the end of the fourteenth century. The Mullsjö Runes came to light in Sweden in 1953, and, from the style of the lettering, were at first thought to have been inscribed in about AD 1000. However, translation put paid to speculation that they were an important archaeological discovery. The inscription turned out not to be in any Scandinavian language but in modern English. Part of it said 'Joe Doakes went East 1953. He discovered Europe. Holy smoke!'

Mullsjö is by no means the only runic riddle which has proved to be less than it seems. In the United States, controversy has raged over the so-called 'Kensington Rune Stone' for almost a century. It began when a farmer named Olof Ohman from Kensington, Minnesota, claimed to have found the stone in the roots of a tree. Its message, if genuine, would demote Christopher Columbus from being the discoverer of the New World to the status of a Johnny-come-lately. The runes said:

8 Swedes and 22 Norwegians on an exploration journey from Vinland westward. We had our camp by 2 rocky islets one day's journey north of this stone. We were out fishing one day. When we came home we found 10 men red with blood and dead. AVM save us from evil. We have 10 men by the sea to look after our ships, 14 days' journey from this island. Year 1362.

Although the stone has had its champions over the years – one writer who acquired it discussed the stone in no fewer than four books – it is now thought to have been a good-humoured hoax perpetrated by farmer Ohman. Not that such conclusions have bothered the residents of Alexandria, Minnesota, where a huge replica of the Kensington Stone was unveiled in Runestone Memorial Park in 1951.

While we are on the subject, one last runic curiosity – although this is not so much a case of forgery as of mistaken identity.

At Runamo in the Blekinge district of southern Sweden, strange rune-like carvings in a 'snake' of rock running through a forest clearing, have fascinated people since earliest times. As long ago as the twelfth century, King Valdemar the Great of Sweden convened a royal commission to copy the runes on to wooden tablets and interpret them. In this they failed miserably, and it was not until 1833 that Finn Magnusson, a distinguished professor from the University of Copenhagen, announced he had found the answer. He claimed the runes formed an epic poem about the battle of Bravalla, fought in ancient times but about which little is known.

Magnusson's triumph, however, was short-lived. He rapidly came under fire from scientists, and by 1844 all the professor's theories had been exploded: the 'runes' had, in fact, been written by Mother Nature. They were natural flaws in the rock!

Jane Austen's marriage lines

The register of banns and marriages for the years 1755 to 1812 for the parish of the English village of Steventon, Hampshire, contains two fake entries written by the novelist Jane Austen (1775–1817). The giveaway is that they are to be found on the page on which sample entries are provided for inexperienced clergymen, and not amongst the lists of real people.

It is quite obvious that the entries were made as a joke, for Jane Austen names a different 'husband' in each section. In the first, devoted to the calling of banns, she claims that her intended is one Henry Frederic

Howard Fitzwilliam of London. In the second marriage entry, he appears as Edmund Arthur Willliam Mortimer of Liverpool. And to complicate matters even further, not only have the 'bride' and 'groom' signed themselves 'Jack Smith' and 'Jane Smith, late Austen,' but Jack and Jane are also down as witnesses!

A reconstructed relic

Regrettably, even religious relics are not immune to a touch of fakery, although it is often well-intentioned. The revelation, in October 1988, that the Turin Shroud could not have been used to wrap the body of Christ but was a medieval fake is a celebrated case in point. Another concerns the body of St Clare of Assisi who died in 1260. The Saint's remains were rediscovered during improvements to her church, Santa Chiara, in 1850. She had weathered the centuries well, so her preserved body was dressed and put on display, along with some of her undergarments and hair shaved from her head when she became a nun.

In 1986 a team of scientists was summoned to Assisi. It was led by the head of the Vatican Museum's Egyptian department, an expert on mummification. The reason for the emergency was soon obvious: the saint was distintegrating. One reason for this became apparent when her skeleton was examined: of its 208 bones, only 57 were real. The rest were fakes made of beeswax and resin. The body had begun to decay because the clothes in which it had been dressed had proved to be a breeding-ground for micro-organisms.

A little gallery of fakes

In the art world, forgery is all too common, and, for the gallery or private collector who has paid good money, by no means amusing. However, the revelation in 1987 that some museums in America had been unwittingly displaying fake 'pre-Columbian' sculptures did produce a few chuckles. The 'treasures' turned out to have been knick-knacks mass-produced in the 1950s and sold for $18 each!

There was intense excitement in the Italian art world in 1984 when three stone heads thought to have been sculpted by the great Modigliani were recovered from the bed of a canal. The search had been organised by the curator of a museum which was mounting a centenary exhibition of the artist's works. He had heard a rumour that Modigliani, in a fit of depression, had dumped some of his masterpieces in the water in 1909.

The euphoria was soon punctured when three students from Leghorn, the artist's birthplace, confessed that they had dashed off the sculptures in just four hours with hammers, chisels and an electric drill. Yet at first few people believed them, and the hoax was only accepted when the three 'Modiglianis' repeated the process in front of the television cameras.

Hitler, Howard Hughes and Mickey Spillane

What, you may ask, have they got in common? Answer: books said to have been written by them have turned out to be fakes. Although literary forgery is less common than the faking of works of art, its consequences are often more far-reaching. Millions of pounds have been involved in the printing and distribution of such books, and many thousands of readers have devoted hours of reading to them.

The greatest prize for a literary forger is to sell the 'memoirs' of a major historical figure or, failing that, of a famous recluse. In 1968 the London *Sunday Times* acquired the rights to what appeared to be the diaries of the Italian dictator Mussolini. The newspaper handed over a six-figure sum before finding that they had bought a forgery: the work of an Italian woman and her 84-year-old mother.

Three years later, writer Clifford Irving managed to convince an American publisher that his 'autobiography' of the billionaire recluse Howard Hughes was the real thing. While the so-called *Hitler Diaries*, palmed off on a German magazine group in 1983, proved once again that the most hard-headed of publishers and historians can be misled by their enthusiasm for world exclusives and new discoveries.

Far more curious is the case of a book called *Hitler Speaks*, published in Britain in 1939. It purported to be a record of conversations between Hitler and an otherwise obscure regional politician called Hermann Rauschning. Historians seized on *Hitler Speaks* as important raw material, and the conversations it contains are quoted in many war histories and biographies of the dictator. Yet in 1985 the German *Die Zeit* exposed the book as a fake. The long conversations, it said, had never taken place: Rauschning had derived the Fuhrer's 'thoughts' from speeches, articles and Hitler's own *Mein Kampf*.

Yet despite this revelation, there were few red faces amongst historians. Rauschning had undoubtedly written the book for money, but somehow he had succeeded in capturing the very essence of Hitler's character and philosophy. As one observer wrote:

> His work still brings before us the most convincing Hitler that we have. How could this be, if he made it all up? Rauschning emerges in his writings as a man who had read and thought a lot and whose reading and thinking were allied to something close to imaginative genius – imaginative not simply in the pejorative sense of the forger.... Rauschning's conversations were forged. But his Hitler wasn't.

More amusing, and certainly of less literary and historical significance, was the disclosure that Turkish readers of Mickey Spillane's novels have by no means always been treated to the punchy prose of the master himself. Such was the demand for Spillane novels in Turkey in the 1950s that a writer called Afif Yesari was hired by a publisher to fake a few. Mr Yesari discharged his task with extraordinary energy and rapidly turned out some 200 Mickey Spillane imitations, which still left him enough time to write other books, in the names of other successful authors, such as Edgar Rice Burroughs and Agatha Christie! Sadly these now highly collectable curiosities are hard to find, and Mr Yesari himself has apparently had to forage for them in second-hand bookshops.

A giant hoax

The curators of the Farmers' Museum and Village Crossroads at Cooperstown, New York, USA, are actually proud to acknowledge that one of their most prized exhibits is an out-and-out fake. For the Farmers' Museum is the last resting-place of the Cardiff Giant, one of the most famous forgeries in American history.

The discovery of the Giant, which is 10 feet $4\frac{1}{2}$ inches tall and weighs 2,999 pounds, caused a sensation in the autumn of 1869. It had been unearthed on a farm at Cardiff, New York State, and the farmer, William C. Newell, made a fortune by putting it on show. There was no lack of doctors, scientists and fossil experts willing to pronounce the 'body' genuine: one even drilled into the Giant's head and claimed to have noticed all kinds of interesting things about his brain.

Yet the Giant turned out to have been a hoax organised by a relation of Newell's called George Hull. Hull had fallen out with a fundamentalist preacher over the interpretation of the Biblical line, 'There were giants in the earth in those days.' The preacher had asserted that every word in the

Bible was literally true; the sceptical Hull, however, was determined to make a fool of him.

Hull had the Giant carved secretly in Chicago – it bore a marked resemblance to him – and buried it by night on Newell's farm. The hoax achieved its object in spectacular fashion. By the end of the year, when the truth had emerged, the preacher was discredited, Newell had made plenty of money, and all America was amused.

The Schleswig Turkey

Finally, here's the story of the Schleswig Turkey, a really preposterous fake. It was revealed in the early 1950s, when a German painter named Lother Malskat was involved in a famous art forgery case. In the course of his confessions, Malskat said that, while restoring some medieval murals in Schleswig Cathedral before the Second World War, he had noticed that part of one of the paintings contained an outline which reminded him of a turkey. He found the temptation to draw one in quite irresistible: the only problem was that the murals were supposed to date from long before the discovery of the turkey by Europeans exploring the New World.

But nobody noticed the anachronistic bird. And when Malskat confessed, some experts, not to be outdone, opined that the official date for the discovery of turkeys just had to be wrong, and that they must have been brought to Europe by earlier explorers so that they could pose for the Schleswig murals!

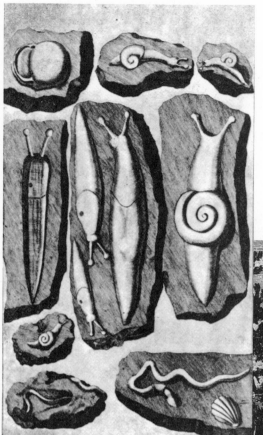

Dr Beringer's *Lügensteine*. Hoaxers planted these 'lying stones' containing preposterous 'fossils' to r the reputation of a distinguished German academ

Many hopefuls tried in vain to decipher the meaning of Sweden's Runamo runes without realizing that they had been 'written' by Mother Nature.

INSIGNE COMITATUS BLEKINGIÆ.

—————————————— ᘒ·ᘒ ——————————————

34

Stone Me!

Stones may often *look* boring, but some have remarkable properties. They can make music, for instance, or move of their own accord. A few have even been thought to have housed living creatures for decades in some kind of mysterious suspended animation. Seekers after the curious cannot afford to leave any stone unturned.

The stones that lied

Two strange stones in the University Museum at Oxford are relics of a celebrated eighteenth-century hoax which ruined the reputation of a distinguished German academic.

Dr Johann Bartholemew Adam Beringer was Dean of the Faculty of Medicine at the University of Würzburg and an avid collector of shells, minerals and fossils. In 1725 it seemed that his ambition to astonish the world by finding remarkable and hitherto unknown types of fossils would be fulfilled. For that year three young fossil-hunters brought him what appeared to be a sensational collection of stones which they claimed to have found on a hill at Eibelstadt near Würzburg.

The stones appeared to contain extraordinary fossils. To describe them as being of a hitherto unknown type would be an understatement. There were comets, flowers with bees in the act of harvesting pollen, petrified inscriptions – some of them in Hebrew – even a spider's web complete with fly-catching spider. Little was known about the origins of fossils at the time, and Beringer was well and truly fooled.

In 1726, he reported his findings and theories in a book called *Litho-*

graphiae Wirceburgensis which contained illustrations of the stones. When rumours spread that he had been hoaxed, Beringer steadfastly continued to argue that most, if not all, the 'fossils' were genuine.

The culprits, however, were soon unmasked. They were two jealous academics who had set out to ruin the gullible doctor because they disliked his manner towards them. They had employed one of the 'finders' to finish off stones they had carved in secret and then present them to Beringer.

Apart from the Oxford *Lügensteine*, a few dozen of the 2,000 in Beringer's original collection survived into this century in collections in the universities of Würzburg and Bonn.

The original rock music

'Musical' rocks – you can 'play' them by tapping them with another stone or with a hammer – can be found throughout the world. At least one bizarre 'rock' concert has been held: in June 1890, a certain Dr J.J. Ott entertained the Buckwampum Historical Society in Bucks County, Pennsylvania, USA, to several numbers played on stones. The ringing tones the doctor produced could apparently be heard clearly over those from the accompanying brass band.

Bucks County boasts extensive rocky areas, known to geologists as *felsenmeer* or 'stone seas', and many of the stones to be found there can be made to produce musical notes. Over the years, fascinated travellers have reported to the scientific journals other discoveries of similar strange 'instruments'.

In 1873, for example, Richard J. Nelson wrote to *Nature* to say that he had often found musical stones on walks near Kendal in the English Lake District.

> They are generally thin flat weather-beaten stones, of different sizes and peculiar shapes, which when struck with a piece of iron or another stone, produce a distinct musical tone, instead of the dull heavy leaden sound of any ordinary stone. [He added that he knew] gentlemen who possess sets of eight stones which are said to produce, when struck, a distinct octave.

From Ch'ufu, China, the birthplace of Confucius, Alfred Tingle described 'three very fine examples of "sounding stones", or "stone gongs" as they are sometimes called'. One formed the cover of an incense dish in the tomb of Confucius's grandson. According to Mr Tingle's account, 'when struck with a stick, or even with the knuckles, it rings as though it were bronze.'

Inside the town's temple a stone tablet and two pillars also produced pleasing notes.

Other 'rock gongs' have been discovered at Shira, Kufena and Katsina in Nigeria and also in Uganda. There are several, too, in France, including two at St Bieuzy in Brittany; while the existence of the 'Hotel des Pierres Sonnantes' at Le Guildo indicates the appeal of the local musical boulders as a tourist attraction.

But why are some stones 'musical' and others not? In the 1960s a team of scientists investigated the ringing rocks of Bucks county, Pennsylvania, so memorably played by Dr J. J. Ott. They noticed that when the stones were broken with a hammer, chips flew off through the air at great speed, 'sometimes flying past one's ear with a humming sound'. This suggested that the rocks were under some internal stress. Experiment confirmed the theory. The scientists sawed the ends off the stones and, with delicate strain gauges, measured how much they 'relaxed'. Those which did not produce musical notes showed no release of internal stress, but those that did showed rapid 'relaxation'.

More experiments were needed to establish the cause of the stress. The scientists found that weathering altered the minerals in the rock. The 'new' mineral had a greater volume than the old and its attempts to burst through the stone's outer 'skin' caused the stress to build up. Finally, the environment of the rock field was an important factor: the 'gongs' were all in comparatively dry places where the mineral changes were slow.

Too heavy for the heavies

Since the turn of the century, Scotland's 800-pound Dinnie Stones have been a frustrating challenge for the beefy athletes who specialise in the heavyweight events at Highland games. They may be able to toss the caber or throw the hammer with relative ease, but none of them has been able to carry both stones at the same time since the day one of their predecessors, Donald Dinnie, picked them up and strolled across a bridge at Potarch in Aberdeenshire.

In September 1987 three of the world's strongest men, Bill Kazmaier of the USA, Geoff Capes of Britain and Jon Pall Sigmarsson of Iceland, failed the challenge which had been organised by a television programme. Said the producer, 'Our guys never even came close. The boys say it is impossible to walk with the stones because of their shape and weight difference.'

Death Valley's moving stones

On the bed of Racetrack Playa, a dried-up lake at the edge of California's Death Valley, stones seem to travel under their own power. This curious phenomenon, known to occur on other *playas* in the area, was not explained until two Californian geologists began a study in 1968.

The stones gouge out long tracks in the surface – a mixture of mud and clay: some of them curve and loop for hundreds of yards. Yet how could rocks weighing as much as 600 pounds move such distances without help from people or animals?

After seven years of careful observation, the geologists, Robert P. Sharp and Dwight L. Carey, came up with a plausible explanation. They found the secret lay in a combination of ground and weather conditions: a wet and slippery *playa* after rain, plus strong winds. Dr Carey has described what he believes happens:

> The wind is able to pick up the rock and start it moving. It pushes aside the very slippery mud and slides along on the firm surface. It's probably moving a couple of feet per second as it rides off across the *playa*, and after a hundred, two hundred feet of movement, or sometimes just a very little movement, the stone will eventually come to rest as the wind dies down. I believe it's basically changes in the wind during the time when the rock is moving that cause the stone trails to be so variable.

Going round in circles

Stonehenge on Salisbury Plain in Wiltshire must rank amongst the world's greatest curiosities. Yet the other thousand or so stone circles scattered throughout the British Isles and northern France are no less curious in their way.

We are not going to list them here. Instead, we will concentrate upon a few circles and standing stones which have become surrounded by the trappings of more recent 'civilisation'.

Two Scottish circles, at Lundin Links, Fife, and Ferntower, Perthshire, are on golf courses. Another, also in Perthshire, is in the garden of a cottage called Tigh-na-Ruaich. Perthshire, in fact, seems to have incorporated more circles into the modern landscape than any other county, for there is also one set amidst the houses of Greystanes Close in the town of Scone. Aviemore, Inverness-shire, has one in a similar situation.

Grey Croft, Cumbria, now stands in the shadow of a twentieth-century wonder, Calder Hall nuclear power station.

The circle at Midmar, Aberdeenshire, is a feature of the village churchyard. Another 'Christianised' prehistoric stone is Britain's tallest megalith at Rudston church in Yorkshire. At St Duzec, Penvern, Brittany, France, a huge menhir, over eight metres high, erected in prehistoric times, was decorated with Christian carvings and crowned with a cross when the nearby chapel was built in 1674. A similar 'converted' menhir stands at Hameau de Rungleo near Brest. In fact, great efforts were made by the Bretons to integrate pagan remains into their more modern religious framework. Many ancient stones stand within churchyard walls. At Sept-Saints, a village near Plouaret, they even built their church over a chambered prehistoric tomb, and at St Mirel, thirty kilometres from Dinan, a chapel was erected between two giant menhirs.

Rock of Inspiration

One of the most famous hymns in the English language, *Rock of Ages*, was inspired by a rock at Burrington Combe in Somerset. It was here that the hymn's writer, the Rev. Augustus Toplady, sheltered during a thunderstorm, and began to compose

> Rock of Ages, cleft for me,
> Let me hide myself in thee . . .

Holy stones and stones with holes

Some stones are thought to have magical or holy powers to heal the sick. There are several in the British Isles. The Men-an-Tol near St Just, Cornwall, was thought to have curative properties if a sick person crawled through it. Rickets, particularly, it was said, stood no chance against the magic of the stone. According to local legend, a child passed through the Long Stone at Minchinhampton, Gloucestershire, would be cured of any ailment. The same properties have been claimed by the Irish for the Speckled Stone at Tobernavean, Sligo.

Other stones with holes, at Wolverhampton, Barnstaple in Devon, and Retford in Nottinghamshire, were used for sealing bargains. When a deal

One of the strange, apparently self-propelled stones of California's Death Valley. Scientists have cracked the mystery, but the phenomenon continues to fascinate visitors who penetrate the far reaches of the a

ᴠᴇ Sick people who clamber through the Speckled Stone at Tobernavean in County Sligo, Eire, are
to benefit from its magical healing properties.

ᴏᴡ This glistering boulder, balanced precariously upon the edge of a precipice on a Burmese mountain,
ɪ object of pilgrimage for Buddhist monks.

was struck, the parties to a contract shook hands through the hole to confirm agreement.

The golden boulder

Near the town of Kyakito in Burma, an extraordinary Buddhist shrine in the form of a gigantic golden boulder appears to be about to topple from the summit of a 3,000-foot mountain. Yet the local monks have such confidence in its permanence that they have built a pagoda right on top, to house a relic of the Buddha.

35

Oddball buildings

Follies and weird buildings abound. Here's our – tiny – selection from the vast number of eccentric constructions the world has to offer. Some were built simply to satisfy a whim, others just grew, yet others were designed decoratively to disguise utilitarian functions. In the course of our travels in America we remember marvelling at examples of uninhibited architecture (and broad-minded planning laws), which included a Glass Slipper Motel, shaped like Cinderella's shoe though made of blue concrete not glass, and a record store disguised as a packing-case.

One of us has childhood memories of the 'House in the Clouds' which dominates the village of Thorpeness in Suffolk. Thorpeness was designed at the beginning of the twentieth century as a holiday resort for the genteel rich, and its builders were unwilling to allow the look of the place to be disfigured by the tower needed to supply the houses with water. They solved the problem with an amusing piece of architectural sleight-of hand. They built a five-storey dwelling in the tower, while the tank itself sat at the very top, and was disguised as a cheerful little house!

The 'house with eyes' in Waltersdorf, East Germany, is proof that an architect needs do little to add that distinctive touch. In this case, tiled 'eyelids' over the windows were all that was necessary.

California boasts at least two buildings whose function can be guessed at a glance. In Los Angeles, a gigantic terrier-like creature stands out against a brown cabin – it's the Dog House bar of course. And even more elaborate are the offices of United Equipment in Turlock, California. They had one side of their offices designed in the shape of their most important line – a caterpillar bulldozer. The other side of the building is conventional – for California.

In Bristol, Tennessee, a collection of rare stringed musical instruments is housed in a custom-built museum – shaped like a guitar. The colourful building also contains a recording studio and gift shop. Experts call this type of architecture 'duck architecture'. Named after a duck-shaped duck shop built on Long Island in the 1930s, the term refers to buildings shaped like the things on sale inside.

A chain of stores called Best has a policy of erecting attention-grabbing buildings. The one we like, er, best is at Milwaukee, Wisconsin. It looks half-built, yet stocked with merchandise. All an illusion, of course: the store's real walls are made of glass and set six feet back from the fake 'shell'.

Near the airport at Colombo, Sri Lanka, there is a wonderful garage shaped like an aeroplane, erected by a devotee of air travel, and in Durban, South Africa, businessman Dookie Ramdarie built himself a concrete house in the form of a magnificent ocean liner.

And talking of ships, the Japanese have jokily transformed a cruise boat on Lake Hakone near Tokyo so that it now looks like the swans that glide through its waters.

Back to buildings. At Rockport, Massachusetts, there is a house – at 52 Pigeon Hill – made entirely out of rolled up newspapers. While at Hellam, Pennsylvania, a shop shaped like a shoe was built in 1948 as an advertising stunt by a flamboyant businessman who apparently simply handed an old boot to his architect and told him to get on with the job. The shoe has recently been restored. The living room is in the toe and there is an ice cream parlour in the instep. The men who commissioned the house, shoe store tycoon Mahlon N. Haines, is portrayed as 'Haines The Shoe Wizard' on the stained glass front door. At Lupton, Arizona, the Tomahawk Indian Store is a huge teepee.

But the prize for America's most charming crazy construction must go to Lucy the Margate Elephant at Margate, New Jersey. Lucy is a former hotel built in the 1880s. And of mammoth size, as you'd expect: sixty-five feet high and seventy-five feet from the tip of her trunk to her tail. There are five rooms inside her body, reached by staircases in her hind legs. A sixth room which acts as a kind of observatory, is situated in the howdah on Lucy's back.

The British tended to build oddball buildings to disguise their often mundane functions. Typical is a little mock-Tudor house in London's Soho Square – in reality a garden tool-shed put up in the 1870s.

In the North of England, not all industrialists were content to settle for utilitarian factory buildings. Few are more exotic than Marshall's flax mill in Leeds which was constructed in the Egyptian style – a temple to enterprise indeed. In its heyday, however, the factory's greatest curiosity was not so much its exotic Egyptian detail, more suited to the banks of

designers of the elegant English
...ay resort of Thorpeness went to
...t lengths to keep reality at bay. This
...se in the Clouds, which conceals the
...er supply, is a prime example of their
...gination and ingenuity.

...ty outlook: the 'House with Eyes' at
...ltersdorf, Germany.

the Nile than the Leeds–Liverpool canal, but its flat roof. It was insulated with earth to ensure that the flax was worked at an even temperature, enabling Mr Marshall to combine those two Yorkshire principles of 'Where There's Muck There's Brass' and 'Waste Not Want Not' to commercial advantage: he grazed sheep on the grass that sprang up there.

Not far away, in Halifax, stands an industrial relic with rather more claim to be described as a folly. Wainhouse tower was completed in 1874: Mr Wainhouse intended it to act as the chimney for his dye works, and, since he was a keen environmentalist, he decreed that not only was it to look more ornamental than run-of-the-mill smokestacks, but it should also be so tall that the burgers of Halifax would be untroubled by its smoke. As it turned out, the tower never served as a chimney because Wainhouse sold the dye works before it was finished. For a *really* grandiose attempt at disguise, you have to visit the Scottish town of Oban, Argyllshire. The place is dominated by a replica of the Colosseum in Rome. Known as 'McCaig's Folly', it was planned to house a museum and art gallery, but was sadly never completed.

36

Treasures in trouble

In July 1987, a Japanese nightclub owner restored to the people of France an essential relic of their history: a hat which had once belonged to the Emperor Napoleon, and was said to be worth at least £375,000. The hat had been acquired by the nightclub owner's father, now dead, who had given instructions for its return in his will. To historians, the gesture was welcome but ironic, for Napoleon was one of the greatest looters in history. He stuffed the Louvre and the provincial art galleries of France with trophies stripped from the treasure-houses of his conquests, including the Vatican. Even the four bronze horses from the basilica of San Marco in Venice were carted off, despite the protests of the Venetians. (Admittedly, the horses had been, as it were, 'on the road' a long time. Originally from ancient Greece, they had probably 'stopped off' in Rome before reaching Constantinople from where they were eventually plundered by the Venetians in 1204.)

Napoleon, of course, was simply behaving like many other conquerors before and since. In fact, large-scale looting of occupied countries was common until the twentieth century (and was revived by the Nazis in the Second World War). In many cases, the purloined trophies of victory were returned in defeat, but international disputes over the ownership of some treasures continue to this day.

Losing their marbles

The wrangle over Britain's most notorious 'loot', the Elgin Marbles, began at the beginning of the nineteenth century, soon after they had been cut from the Parthenon in Athens by the Scottish peer. The Marbles were not the spoils of war: Elgin maintained he simply wished to protect them from the Turks who ruled Greece and were no respecters of her ancient glories. He took about half the temple's sculptures and they are now in London's British Museum. Despite regular appeals for the Marbles' return, to which many luminaries from Lord Byron to Melina Mercouri have lent their voices, Lord Elgin's trophies seem destined to remain in what Thomas Hardy called

> this gaunt room
> Which sunlight shuns, and sweet Aurora
> but enters cold.

And if, at some future date, the British Museum was to change its mind, London would not be entirely Marble-less: Elgin's secretary William Hamilton took casts which form a frieze in his old house in the King's Road.

Meanwhile in Athens, it was announced in 1988, a room at the new Acropolis Museum has been left empty – to house the Elgin Marbles if they are ever returned.

Bearding the authorities

Occasionally, museums do return treasures to representatives of their former owners. In 1987, for example, Washington's Smithsonian Institution handed back Indian artefacts claimed by the Zuni Pueblo tribe of New Mexico.

Usually, any hand-back takes a long time to negotiate and carry out. It took decades for Denmark to return a huge collection of Icelandic sagas to the country from which they came.

The Danes acquired the sagas in 1730 by an historical accident. They formed part of a collection of 1,800 manuscripts owned by an Icelandic scholar named Arni Magnusson who became a professor at the University of Copenhagen. On his death in 1730, Magnusson bequeathed the collection to the university, and it was not until 1965 that agreement was reached between Denmark and Iceland for its return. A deadline of 1996 was set for the completion of the transfer: this would allow the Danes time to copy and restore the fragile documents. By 1991, with three-quarters of the 1,800 manuscripts back in the land of their origin, the transfer was reported to be going according to schedule.

But such agreements between nations are rare. In the 1980s, speculation that a deal had been struck over one curious artefact in the British Museum proved to be unfounded.

According to a story given prominence in the Egyptian press, the British Museum had agreed to return part of the beard of the Great Sphinx of Giza to the Egyptians on long-term loan. In exchange, the Egyptians would be lending the body of a statue of the jackal-god Anubis – an idea apparently welcomed by the museum since it already owned the head. The beard fragment, a stone block some two feet high with plaits cut into it, was found in the sand beneath the Sphinx by an Italian naval officer in 1818.

However, no such deal was ever struck, and the British Museum told us: 'It hasn't gone back on loan, and the Egyptians haven't put in a request for permanent restitution.'

Even British subjects have had cause to object to the British Museum's right, enshrined in an Act of Parliament, to keep its collection in perpetuity. In 1986 the Rev. Cedric Catton, vicar of Exning, Suffolk, discovered that a curious piece of medieval church plate, used for holding Communion bread, which had been dug up close to his church probably in 1844, was languishing in one of the Museum's store-rooms. The value of the Exning Pyx, as it was named, lay not in the brass from which it was fashioned but in its rarity – only two or three other British examples of its vintage are known. When the vicar asked for its return, the answer was 'No': officials pointed out that a new law would have to be passed to allow restitution.

Said Mr Catton:

I can think of a lot worse use for Parliament's time. The idea of persuading Parliament to let us have our pyx back appeals to my sense of being English. I think we have a historic right to it.

Pocketing the Koh-i-Noor

Calls have also been made for the return to India of the Koh-i-Noor diamond, the 110–carat stone in the Queen Mother's crown. It was surrendered to Queen Victoria by the Maharajah of Lahore at the annexation of the Punjab in 1849. In fact, the diamond almost never made it to Queen Victoria's jewel-box for it was given to the Viceroy, John Lawrence, to deliver. Lawrence absent-mindedly left it in the pocket of his coat when it went to the wash. Fortunately, when he inquired of his *dhobi*, 'Did you find a piece of glass in my pocket?' the *dhobi* produced it immediately, ensuring that the greatest stone of the Jewel in the Crown could become a jewel in the English crown.

The Mafeking gun

In 1987 the town of Mafeking, now a suburb of Mmabatho, capital of the South African black homeland of Bophuthatswana, asked for its gun back. The gun was a home-made cannon, run up by railway engineers during the siege of Mafeking in the Boer War of 1899–1902. After the relief of Mafeking in May 1900, Robert Baden-Powell, the British soldier who had commanded the besieged garrison and withstood the attacks of the Boers, shipped the gun back to Britain. Once again, Queen Victoria was the recipient of this colonial booty. It is now in London's Woolwich Arsenal.

Casanova's bones

In 1987, an official of the Venice city council, Mr Augusto Salvadori, put forward one of the strangest restitution claims on record. The plan was to get back the remains of one of Venice's most notorious citizens, Giovanni Giacomo Casanova. Casanova is buried at Dux near Bratislava, Czechoslovakia, where he took refuge after being drummed out of his native city for immoral behaviour. It was thought that the 'presence' of the great lover's remains might add spice to the annual Venice carnival.

The £80,000 stool

Sometimes the chance for a nation to reclaim its heritage occurs in the saleroom. One such opportunity occurred when a little wooden stool carved from a single piece of wood was bought for £80,000 at Christie's by the Tahiti Museum. The price reflected the stool's importance in Tahitian history, for it belonged to the first Polynesian ever to visit Britain, a man named Omai. Omai made the long voyage to London in 1774 in the hope of persuading the king to help him reclaim land which had been seized by his enemies.

In Britain, Omai's arrival created a sensation. He was received at Court and portrayed by Sir Joshua Reynolds. A sketch by another artist, Nathaniel Dance, actually shows Omai with the stool sold at Christie's. Omai gave it to the family with whom he stayed in England, along with his slippers and some wooden clubs. All these relics of the exotic visitor were sent for sale by a descendant of Omai's original hosts.

A reminder of the international disputes that can arise today over souvenirs acquired by travellers and sailors in the heyday of the British Empire, came in May 1988 when the planned sale of the preserved head of a Maori warrior was halted after protests from New Zealand.

The head was one of many throughout the world – the Maoris used to exchange them for weapons until the practice was forbidden in the 1820s – and had been expected to fetch between £6,000 and £10,000. The outcome of the controversy was a decision to send the head back to New Zealand for a dignified burial.

37

Oh what a curious war!

The scars of war are difficult to erase, not only from the minds of the participants but also from the landscape on which defences have been erected and battles fought. The oddest reminders of conflict survive long after the cessation of hostilities, often in the strangest places. For example, a prehistoric passage-grave near Ploemeur in Brittany, France, was used as an emplacement for anti-aircraft guns in the Second World War and not restored until the mid-1970s. In Britain and Ireland, many of the Martello towers built between 1804 and 1812 to repel the expected Napoleonic invasion (which never came) have been converted into homes. As readers of *Ulysses* will know, author James Joyce lived for a time in one near Dublin, while the Martello Tower at Aldeburgh, Suffolk, can be rented as a holiday home. One result of the reunification of Germany has been an increase in tourists to Germany's most 'escape-proof' wartime prison camp, Colditz Castle. In 1990, one enterprising travel company was offering a day trip from London. But so far a scheme to convert the castle into a luxury hotel has not been put into action.

Eden restored

A Second World War prison camp in England has already been restored as a tourist and educational attraction. POW Camp 83 near Malton, Yorkshire, had been left virtually unaltered after its last inmates returned home in 1948. Known locally as 'Eden Camp', the place had housed German and Italian prisoners. Sympathetically done up and still surrounded by its barbed-wire fence, the camp now provides what its owners call 'a civilian wartime experience,' with exhibits of memorabilia, war movies running in the cinema, puppets of Vera Lynn and Gracie Fields miming the troops' favourites in a mock-up of a 1940s village hall, air-raid shelters, and, on the sound system, all the familiar explosions, bangs and crashes of the Second World War.

Carve his name with pride

Some mementoes of war were created far from the front line. For example, for more than forty years, one of Britain's most eminent peers, the Marquess of Hertford, was intrigued by a message carved on a beech tree on his estate. It read 'R.J. US Army 1944'. But who was R.J.? When the tree began to die, the Marquess launched a search for the missing carver, so that the inscribed piece of bark could be presented to him. 'R.J.', it turned out, was one Robert Johnson of Carthage, North Carolina. He had made the carving while recovering from wounds on the estate where an emergency hospital had been established.

In another English wood, near the Building Research Station at Garston, near Watford, Hertfordshire, lies a relic of one of the most spectacular of all the RAF's bombing raids and a weird monument to the ingenuity of Britain's wartime 'boffins'. It is a model dam used by the legendary Dr Barnes Wallis to perfect the 'bouncing bomb' with which the Ruhr Dams were destroyed by the famous 'Dambusters' in 1943.

Jacob's head

The head of a heroic goose is carefully preserved amongst the battle honours of Britain's Coldstream Guards at their London regimental head-quarters. The goose was named Jacob and he earned the golden collar, which he still wears, protecting the soldiers against surprise attack from Canadian rebels in Quebec in 1837. Whenever the enemy approached, Jacob would squawk loudly and alert the garrison.

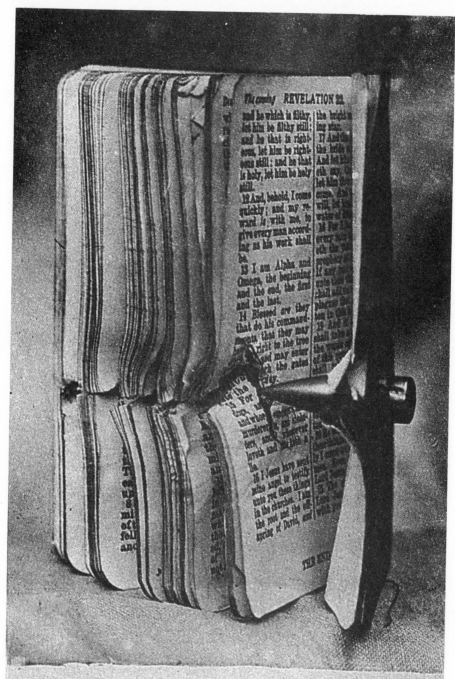

Tough Testament, a postcard commemorating a British soldier's miraculous escape from death in the First World War.

Curious corners of a foreign field

Poignant reminders of the massive casualties of the Battle of the Somme in 1916 still surface beneath farm ploughs in the fields near Albert in France. Human bones, fragments of rifles, even unexploded bombs and shells bring home the scale of the slaughter.

The bullet and the bible

An extraordinary First World War curiosity recently appeared in an exhibition of old postcards at Britain's National Museum of Photography. The postcard shows a copy of the New Testament with a bullet through its cover, and, beneath the photograph, this extraordinary story:

THIS TESTAMENT SAVED THE LIFE OF PTE W. HACKET 1ST WOR REGT AT ARMENTIERES AUG 20 1915 NOW IN 2ND GEN EASTERN HOSPITAL DYKE RD BRIGHTON. BULLET PASSING THROUGH OUTER COVER AND ALL THE LEAVES AND STOPPED AT THE LAST PAGE.

The First Emperor's road

The lost military road of the first Emperor of China was located in 1985 – after two months' footslogging by a Chinese painter named Jin Zhilin and one of his students Sun Xiangwu. Before the rediscovery, the history of the road was well known. It had been built by Emperor Qin Shi Huang Di in the last two years of his reign, 212–210 BC, as a defence against the Xiongnu Huns, but fell out of use in the fifteenth century. Jin and Sun, however, found that, although the roadway itself had disappeared, many relics of times in which the route had flourished still survived to help them retrace it: there were rooftiles from the roadside buildings lying in the fields, the remains of sacrificial platforms and cuttings through mountainsides. From the undergrowth and the mists of antiquity, an extraordinary engineering feat emerged. It turned out that the Emperor's military road was about thirteen metres wide and 700 kilometres long: yet another of the wonders of the ancient Chinese world, fit to rank along with the Great Wall and the Emperor's terracotta army.

The Maginot Line

The Maginot Line, built by the French between the First and Second World Wars to keep Germany from invading their territory, has proved impregnable – if only to time. The Line, which runs across lonely country-side between Stenay and St Louis in Alsace, is a vast network of under-ground bunkers and tunnels in which French troops were meant to live like submariners. There were operations rooms, telephone exchanges, canteens, hospitals, dormitories, trams to transport soldiers and trains to carry munitions. Today, some of the vast fortresses constructed at strategic points along the Line are tourist attractions, most notably those at Hack-enburg and Schoenenberg.

The cost of constructing what writer John Harris has called 'perhaps the most expensive built folly in all history' is unknown. In the event, the invading Germans simply charged their way through some parts of the Line, bypassed the rest, and finally cut it off from the rest of France.

Once reduced to the status of white elephant, the Maginot Line was forgotten until enthusiasts and tourist authorities began to restore it some forty years later. Visiting the great fortifications is an evocative experience, as John Harris found:

> There is a pervading air of mystery, as if redolent of the Rip Van Winkle legend. This may be because so much is still secret about the place, and if we are unknowing, the experience is not unlike an explorer unexpectedly discovering the ruins of a lost civilisation. If we walk through the high woods we can be brought up short by saucer-shaped metal domes set flat upon the ground; or stumbling through the undergrowth be confronted by a vast, cyclopean-battered wall more than 50 ft high and hundreds of yards long; or we catch our breath at overgrown concrete bunkers, or pillbox forts or casements observing us with blank eyes. We have discovered the ruined city of the Maginot Line.

Strange secrets

Many wartime secrets are kept long after the fighting is over, usually because they could be of use to other nations who might become unfriendly in the future. Gradually, however, some of the curiosities hitherto kept under wraps are being unveiled. Recent examples, all from the Second World War, include:

Inside the Maginot line. Trams transported soldiers and munitions along a vast network of tunnels.

A subterranean factory installed by the Plessey Company in a tunnel of the London underground system between Redbridge, Gants Hill and Wanstead stations on the Central Line. More than 2,000 workers were employed there making components for the aircraft industry. The idea was to protect vital machinery from air raids. The production line does not get in the way of today's commuters, however: it was dismantled after the war and the line restored to London Transport.

An art store inside a mountain called the Manod near Blaenau Ffestiniog, North Wales. Masterpieces from London's National Gallery were kept there in old slate workings.

Another, more serious, use for the board game *Monopoly*. Its British manufacturers, John Waddington's of Leeds, made special sets to help prisoners of war escape. The 'extras' included a compass and maps which were hidden in the board, while real currency took the place of Monopoly money.

Dished!

Finally, one of the strangest sights of the 1980s in England's green and pleasant land. Directly behind an olde worlde cottage called Tudor Thatch in the Hampshire village of Oakhanger, Britain's Ministry of Defence has erected a huge satellite tracking station for a military satellite, producing the kind of contrast between ancient and modern beloved of photographers but not of householders intent upon a quiet life in the country with a beautiful view.

$\backsim$ · $\backsim$

38

Unfinished business . . .

Wars and territorial disputes seldom end tidily. There are treaties still waiting to be drawn up to end conflicts which effectively finished generations ago. For example, the Korean War effectively ended with an armistice in 1953, but despite more than 400 meetings, the Military Armistice Commission still has unfinished business . . .

Scilly hostilities

A war between Holland and the Isles of Scilly off the British coast finally ended in April 1986 – 335 years after the Dutch declared war.

Hostilities began in 1651 after a Dutch raid on the islands' pirates who had been attacking and robbing their ships. The Dutch Admiral ordered the islanders to surrender, and when they refused, he declared war. The Dutch Admiral, in turn, was routed by the British Navy, but no one remembered to formally make peace – until April 1986, when the Dutch authorities agreed to draw up a document to end one of the longest conflicts in history.

Berwick-upon-Tweed, on the border between England and Scotland, is said to have been left out of the provisions of the Treaty of Vienna of 1815. This means its citizens are still technically fighting the Napoleonic Wars! However, another outstanding conflict – the Crimean War – *was* settled in 1966 – after 110 years – when a Soviet official visited the town on a peace mission.

Now you may be wondering why little Berwick should ever have featured in international treaties in the first place. The reason is simple: the borders of Scotland and England changed so often that, at any one time, the authorities found it difficult to remember which country Berwick was in. So the place was regularly singled out for mention when declarations of war were made. The problem was that it was often forgotten when the hostilities were over and the peace treaty was drawn up.

In the West of England, the Mayor of Taunton claimed in 1985 that his town was still awaiting a Royal Pardon after supporting the Duke of Monmouth's attempt to seize the throne – in 1685.

One of the oldest international confrontations of all took no less than 2,131 years to sort out. The great African city of Carthage, in what is now Tunisia, was destroyed by the Romans back in 146 BC. It was not until February 1985 that the descendants of both sides met in Tunis (the remains of Carthage lie beneath one of its suburbs) to forgive – if not forget.

Sometimes long-running problems do get resolved – if only more than a century on. Such was the case with a brass cannon which had been intended for a Battle of Waterloo display in 1817 at Wellington, Somerset, in honour of the eponymous Duke's victory. The cannon not only arrived late but turned out never to have been used in the great battle. The locals were so miffed that they simply left it on the quayside at Exeter. It was finally unveiled in 1985.

In fact, the Napoleonic Wars seem to have been notable for unfinished business. It was not until 1984 that France got round to settling a debt of 45,333 Swiss Francs for damage caused by Napoleon's troops to the town of Bourg St Pierre, Switzerland – in 1800!

1984 was also the year in which the British government finally settled a debt which had been outstanding for 775 years. The creditor was Oxford University, which had been granted compensation of £3.08 per year after local people had damaged its property and helped an undergraduate to murder his mistress in 1209. The University accepted the princely sum of £33.08 in full and final settlement.

Debts are somewhat easier to settle, however, than territorial disputes, as the saga of the Mundat Wood has shown. The problem is that the wood, more than three thousand acres in all, lies on the Franco-German border, on a piece of Alsace which juts into Germany.

By now you won't be at all surprised to hear that an argument over which country owned the wood began in 1805 – in Napoleonic times. The row led to a great deal of metaphorical to-ing and fro-ing for the wood:

• In 1805 it became part of France.

• In 1815, after the Congress of Vienna, it was restored to Germany.

- In 1945, when Alsace-Lorraine was handed back to the French after the Second World War, Wissembourg, the nearest town, asked for the wood back too – but it stayed in Germany.

- In 1949, however, 700 hectares of Mundat Wood were handed over to France.

- In 1962, with the row still rumbling on, a compromise plan was put forward. It would have allowed the French to own the wood but the Germans to retain sovereignty. The French ratified the treaty, but the Bundestag threw it out.

- Settlement was finally reached in 1983, after discussions between President Mitterand of France and Chancellor Kohl of West Germany.

- There are two more curious things about the Mundat Wood. The first is that despite its shifting 'nationality, and the number of wars fought in the region, the water it has traditionally supplied to Wissembourg has never been cut off. The second is that nobody lives there.

39

Last writes

A few last curious things...

Big hopes for smallpox

The world's last reservoir of smallpox, the deadly disease that caused millions of deaths before inoculation finally wiped it out, lies in two phials, one in Russia, the other in the United States.

Should they be destroyed? The debate has been going on ever since 1979, the year the World Health Organisation declared the planet to be smallpox-free, no outbreak having been reported in the previous two years.

Some scientists urge that, despite the danger of keeping the deadly virus, the two phials should be kept, just in case a hostile country decided to use smallpox in germ warfare. But when Dr Keith Dumbell of the University of Cape Town, South Africa, conducted a survey amongst virologists throughout the world, only five of the sixty-one who replied to his questionnaire voted for its retention. Dr Dumbell himself expressed this view in a medical journal: 'To the best of my knowledge, destruction of all remaining laboratory stocks would set the final seal on the attempt to rid the world of this infectious scourge.'

While the argument goes on, the two fatal phials remain on ice – one in a freezer in Moscow, the other in Atlanta, Georgia.

Pierre de Fermat, the Frenchman whose last theorem has frustrated and puzzled his fellow mathematicians for more than 350 years.

Fermat's last theorem

Just as you thought you were coasting to the end of this book, we'd like you to stop, wrap a wet towel around your head and consider Fermat's last theorem.

Pierre de Fermat was a brilliant mathematician who, in 1637, was pondering an equation which arises from Pythagoras's Theorem – the one that states that in a right-angled triangle the square of the hypotenuse equals the sum of the squares of the other two sides. The equation can be written like this:

$$x^2 + y^2 = z^2$$

So if $x = 3$ and $y = 4$, then $z = 5$, the equation works, with x, y and z all whole numbers. But what happens if x, y and z are cubed or raised to the fourth power and beyond? Fermat thought that such equations were impossible to solve for whole numbers, and in 1637 wrote in the margin of a book: 'I have discovered a truly remarkable proof which this margin is too small to contain.'

He then promptly died, the mathematicians have struggled to find that proof ever since. Prizes have even been offered – by the French Académie des Sciences in 1850 (a gold medal and 3,000 Francs) and the University of Göttingen, Germany, in 1908.

In 1988, a Japanese mathematician, Dr Yoichi Miyaoka, offered a new solution. Excitement grew, but as so often in the long saga of Fermat's Last Theorem, it was short-lived. The world still waits for that proof. And nothing, as far as we know, has been done to widen the frustratingly narrow margins of maths books.

Last man out...

Every year in Pine Bluff, Arkansas, a group of First World War veterans meet on Armistice Day and place a bottle of unopened cognac on the table. They drink toasts, talk, and sing the old songs. They then disperse, but not before locking the cognac, unopened, back in its cupboard.

This is the Last Man Club in session.

Now it is down to single figures. The club will go on until there is only one man left to open the cognac and drink it. Cheers.

Illustration
Acknowledgements